# Paris,
## the Second
# Time Around

Dedicated
To my sister...

**Special thanks**

Toni, for her heritage, her enthusiasm, and her precious help.

Michel, Nicolas, Thérèse, Joan, and Fred, for their support.

Carol-Ann de Carolis, Claire Mantoux, Nicole Close, Carole Saturno, Leslie Gogois, Betsy Dribben and Pierre Vellay, for their advice.

And to all our friends who inspired this guide with their endless question: "Would you happen to know a great restaurant near Châtelet?"
The answer is yes!

# Paris, the Second Time Around

The Must-Have Guide

Catherine & Caroline Taret

With Anita Conrade

Dining, bar-hopping, culture, and shopping: **where the Parisians like to go!**

PARIGRAMME

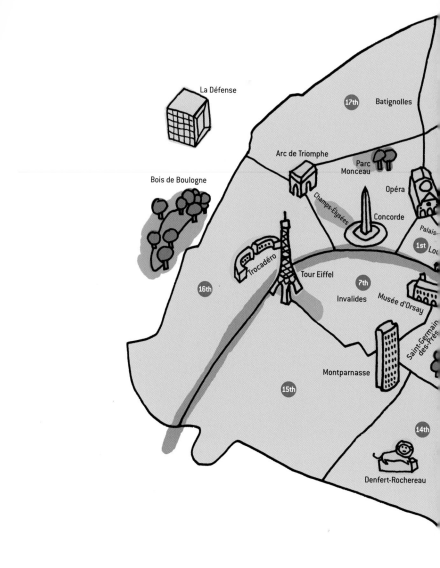

La Défense

17th Batignolles

Arc de Triomphe

Parc Monceau

Opéra

Champs-Élysées

Concorde

Palais-

1st Lou

Bois de Boulogne

Trocadéro

Tour Eiffel

7th

16th

Invalides

Musée d'Orsay

Saint-Germain des-Prés

Montparnasse

15th

14th

Denfert-Rochereau

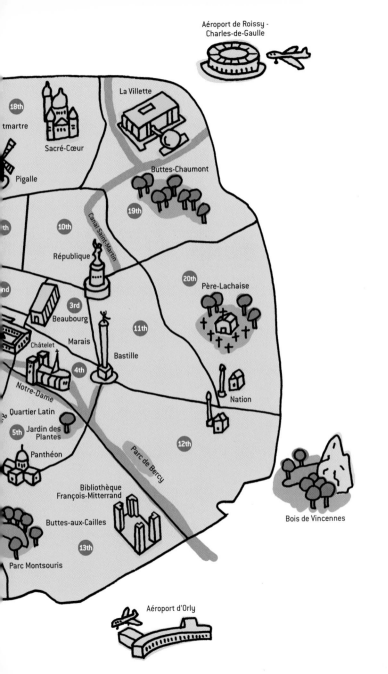

Aéroport de Roissy - Charles-de-Gaulle

La Villette

18th
tmartre

Sacré-Cœur

Pigalle

Buttes-Chaumont

10th

19th

Canal Saint-Martin

République

20th
Père-Lachaise

3rd
Beaubourg

Marais

11th

Châtelet

Bastille

4th

Notre-Dame

Nation

Quartier Latin

5th  Jardin des
Plantes

Panthéon

Parc de Bercy

Bibliothèque
François-Mitterrand

Buttes-aux-Cailles

Bois de Vincennes

12th

13th

Parc Montsouris

Aéroport d'Orly

In English, there is a famous saying: "When in Rome, do as the Romans do." Exploring a city for the first time as a tourist, haven't we all mused, at one point, "What does it feel like when you really live here?" Because we're so busy visiting museums and sightseeing, we seldom get to experience the way the natives live.

We were born in a globetrotting Franco-American family, sharing two cultures and spending most of our vacations house-swapping. We've come to believe that traveling is incomplete when you sleep in a standardized hotel, are unable to chat with the locals, or pack to go home with the same souvenirs sold to millions of others visitors. It's only when you get into a political discussion with a taxi driver, or discover a secret spot that's not in any tour guide, that you start feeling like that new city is a familiar and friendly destination, after all.

This is what our guide is about. Our city is Paris and more visitors come here than anywhere else in the world. You may already have climbed up the Eiffel Tower, looked into the mysterious eyes of the Mona Lisa, and walked down the Champs-Élysées.

About the authors:

**Catherine Taret**

33 years old. 16 years in Paris.
Lives in Les Abbesses.
Her ritual: treating herself to
a "croque-monsieur" with a glass
of rosé wine at the Progrès.
**catherine.taret@gmail.com**

**Caroline Taret**

31 years old. 12 years in Paris.
Lives in Les Batignolles.
Her ritual: walking through the city
listening to her iPod.
**carolinetaret@yahoo.fr**

## How to find a parisian eatery

The Parisian's secret eateries are places with a soul, where the food is great and the ambience warm. Places where neighborhood crowds meet up to satisfy their appetites for both food and chatter, discussing the small and large issues of the day, and "remaking the world." Many of our friends begged us not to review their favorite watering-holes, afraid that the exposure would put an end to their first-name basis relationship with the owner. We've done it anyway... but keep it confidential!

◆ 15 to 30 euros per person, per meal
◆◆ 30 to 50 euros per person, per meal
◆◆◆ over 50 euros per person, per meal

Some of you have even followed in the tracks of the Da Vinci Code or had a drink at the Café de la Paix. Our idea is to show you the real Paris as we know it, and explain how Parisians live in their city from day to day. How? By presenting our favorite addresses and those of our Parisian friends.

By giving you secret insights into Parisian habits, and highlighting their snobbish attitudes (they're Parisian, after all), we hope that you will come to understand this city's inhabitants and realize that even their shortcomings can be chic and endearing.

You might even discover how they live up to their reputation as the best lovers, the greatest cooks, and the most elegant dressers, as well as take a peek at their simple, everyday pleasures (listening to free music at the Fnac or stalking celebrities in supermarkets!).

We won't give you the classic tourist tour: as far as all those famous monuments are concerned, you can't go anywhere in Paris without bumping into one of them anyway!

Because we want to share a slice of life as we live it, we want you to discover "Paris, the Second Time Around."

# 1.
# Opéra and
# Palais-Royal

You've probably toured the gorgeous Opéra house or the Louvre on a previous visit. Good, now you can enjoy the neighborhood as Parisians do: wander around the beautiful gardens of the Palais-Royal, shop on the Rue Saint-Honoré, and discover the up-and-coming nightlife of this central area.

# Parisians' Secret Eateries

## Habemuspapam
FRENCH ◆◆

**13 Rue Monsigny, 2nd • M° Quatre-Septembre • 01 47 42 92 35**
**Monday-Friday 12-2:30 pm and 7:30-11 pm; Saturday 7:30-11 pm**

This somewhat yuppified restaurant is the area's trendiest. Few people know about it, except maybe the after-work set. The food is marvellous: wild mushroom risotto, veggie lasagna, and experimental treats like the rosemary sorbet on the dessert menu. Ambience: colonial-era gentlemen's club, rewired with a New York vibe. Parisians love it!

## ✚ Japanese connection, Rue Sainte-Anne area ◆
### Monday-Saturday 12-2 pm and 7-10 pm

Unagi? Udon? Still wondering what these words mean? Well, you'll love finding out in this particular area of Paris. Between the Opéra Garnier and the Palais-Royal, you'll find many Japanese restaurants that look like canteens: elbow-to-elbow lunch or dinner, quick but tasty food. Tempura, ginger, noodle soups, chicken or pork omelettes on rice... Make your decision when the night is young, because the kitchens close at 10 pm.

Here is a selection of three restaurants, close in menus and prices.

**Sapporo: 37 Rue Sainte-Anne, 2nd • M° Pyramides**
**Aki: 11 bis Rue Sainte-Anne, 2nd • M° Pyramides**
**Katoya: 14 Rue Sainte-Anne, 2nd • M° Pyramides**

### For raw fish lovers
**Foujita: 3 Rue Saint-Roch, 1st • M° Pyramides**
**Foujita 2: 7 Rue du 29-Juillet, 1st • M° Pyramides or Opéra • 01 49 26 07 70**

## Le Grand Colbert
FRENCH ◆◆

**2 Rue Vivienne, 2nd • M° Bourse**
**www.legrandcolbert.fr • 01 42 86 87 88**
**Daily 12 pm-1 am**

Le Grand Colbert is an authentic French brasserie located in the quiet Rue Vivienne, behind the Palais-Royal and next to the Bibliothèque Nationale de France. It's a feast for all the senses: admire the mosaics and frescos that animate the large space filled with white globe lights, listen to the elegant waiters performing their tasks, and ultimately, thrill your taste buds with the typical brasserie seafood platter (fruits de mer), specialty of Paris. *Garçon!*

## Ferdi
WORLD FOOD ◆

**32 Rue du Mont-Thabor, 1st • M° Tuileries**
**01 42 60 82 52**
**Tuesday-Saturday 12-3 pm and 6:30-11 pm**

This little restaurant hidden near the Tuileries is quite popular with style pros: it's mobbed during twice-yearly Fashion Weeks! Ferdi's menu is a sampling  of the world's great recipes, revisited by Ferdi himself and his wife: Mexican mini eggrolls, Spanish combo plates, inspirations from Thailand, and burgers... You may select a couple of dishes and create your own cosmopolitan antipasti. And don't forget to ask Ferdi for his latest wine discovery... The décor is like a journey through the couple's memories.

## Place Numéro Thé
LUNCH & AFTERNOON TEA ◆

**20 Place Dauphine, 1st**
**M° Louvre-Rivoli or Pont-Neuf**
**01 44 07 28 17**
**Monday, Tuesday, Thursday, and Friday for lunch and afternoon snacks (closed for dinner)**

This tiny restaurant is our personal favorite on the enchanting square, located right behind the country's supreme court building. It's filled with legal eagles at lunchtime. The lovely English-speaking owner offers simple and affordable dishes made from fresh ingredients. We enjoyed a warm lentil salad with a poached egg and a delicious apple crumble. Bear in mind the restaurant only opens four days a week at lunch, and closes once all the food has been served.

# Paris fashion eateries

Twice a year, for seven-day intervals, during the famed Fashion Weeks, the Saint-Honoré neighborhood becomes a giant catwalk. Two restaurants are then in great demand, requisitioned for schmoozing, refreshment, and backstage gossip. In these bustling eateries, you'll find hoity-toity fashion editors from the world over, bevies of leggy models, spoiled princesses in Marc Jacobs checking their Blackberries... and waiters who give excellent advice.

Café Marly, the Costes-decorated eatery located right in the Louvre, with a view of the Pei pyramid, is the place to go for celebratory evening glass of champagne. Nibble at an avocado shrimp cocktail to assuage starvation.

However, the new jeunesse dorée tends to opt for a cheeseburger in the magnificent gardens of the Musée des Arts Décoratifs, in the northern wing of the Louvre. Bling-bling girls and their escorts, "jet-lagged from the New York-Paris flight," recharge their depleted batteries here before tripping off to an evening at the Cab or Paris-Paris.

Two more places to go just for the people-watching entertainment available right in the restaurant!

## Café Marly

**Facing the Louvre Pyramid**
**93 Rue de Rivoli, 1st**
01 49 26 06 60
M° Palais-Royal-Musée-du-Louvre
Daily 8-2 am
*€25 menu of the day*

## Le Saut du Loup

**Musée des Arts Décoratifs**
**107 Rue de Rivoli, 1st**
Tel: 01 42 25 49 55
Daily 12 pm-12 am
*€30 menu of the day*

My addresses around Opéra and Palais-Royal

## Aux Lyonnais
FRENCH ◆◆

**32 Rue Saint-Marc, 2nd • M° Richelieu-Drouot**
**01 42 96 65 04**
**Tuesday-Friday for lunch and dinner; Saturday for dinner only**

A great address if you want to discover the world-famous cuisine of France's second city, Lyon, where this type of restaurant is referred to as a "bouchon." Historically, these eateries fed Lyon's silk workers, and to this day, they stand out for their bustling camaraderie. Try the andouilles, cheeses (Saint-Marcellin), hearty meat dishes, and regional wines. Alain Ducasse, one of France's most famous chefs, has elevated this traditional cuisine to an art. It's Lyon in Paris... But if you want to visit Lyon, it's only two hours away by train!

## Chez Jean
FRENCH ◆◆

**8 Rue Saint-Lazare, 9th • M° Saint-Lazare**
**www.restaurantjean.fr • 01 48 78 62 73**
**Monday-Friday 12:15-2:30 pm and 7:45-10:30 pm**

Tell a Parisian you're going out to dinner near the Gare Saint-Lazare, and he's likely to wonder why. He's probably unaware that the area near the train station hides a little treasure. Chez Jean is indeed a nice place to enjoy original cuisine where modernity meets tradition: escargots are on the menu, as well as vegetable soups and veggie plates. Main courses are classic with a twist (lamb, fish) and the desserts end the meal with a chic and colorful flourish (exotic fruits mixed with home-made ice cream, chocolate delights). A dream!

## Chez Pierrot
FRENCH ◆◆

**18 Rue Étienne-Marcel, 2nd • M° Étienne-Marcel**
**01 45 08 00 10**
**Monday-Saturday 12-2:30 pm and 7:15-11 pm**

The neighborhood is busy by day (Rue Étienne-Marcel, on the fringes of the garment district, is the home of the chic Paris blue-jean designers) but quieter by night, making it the perfect place to enjoy a delicious southwestern French meal in this quaint restaurant. Don't hesitate: this authentic regional food is one of our Parisian favorites. What's on the menu? Homemade foie gras, duck confit, Aubrac beef... and chocolate profiterolles for dessert... Did we say anything about a light meal?

# The Night Time is the Right Time

The nightlife in the Opéra-Palais-Royal area is quite chic, with a couple of well-known, upmarket venues (Costes, Le Cab). Our favorite addresses, however, are a couple of blocks away. Near the "Grands Boulevards," funky, edgy crowds gather to worship techno and rock at bars which are like temples to the driving rhythm.

## Delaville Café
DRINKS

**34 Boulevard de Bonne-Nouvelle, 10th • M° Bonne-Nouvelle**
**www.delavillecafe.com • 01 48 24 48 09**
**Monday-Saturday 11 am-2 pm; Sunday 12 pm-2 am**

Parisians used to take long strolls along these "Grands Boulevards," broad avenues once lined with cafes, theaters and cinemas. Today, the Delaville Café attracts crowds thirsty for refreshment (and hungry for the chef's cheeseburgers, among the best in town). It is a historical landmark: an old theater that has come back to life as a trendy, arty bar and restaurant with a great terrace. Traces of the building's past bring instant charm to the visit. The crowd is typical 10th arrondissement: creative types (graphic artists, writers, advertisers, designers) and popular theater lovers.

## Rex Club
DANCING

**5 Boulevard Poissonnière, 2nd • M° Bonne-Nouvelle**
**www.rexclub.com • 01 42 36 61 96**
**From 11:30 pm • Cover charge: €10-15**

One of Paris's great places to dance if you love techno: Laurent Garnier, the legendary French-touch DJ started here! You can't miss the venue, with its white tower and red neon letters. The Rex movie theater hosts premieres and events, while a couple of meters down you'll find the door to the club. Inside, groove to the funky sets being mixed by the many DJs. The layout of the club makes it possible to get up close and personal with the artist, should that appeal to you. This affordable nightspot is emblematic of the way to have fun in the capital: unsophisticated but true.

## Social Club
LIVE MUSIC

**142 Rue Montmartre, 2nd • M° Bourse**
**www.myspace.com/parissocialclub • www.parissocialclub.com**
**From 11 pm • Cover charge: €0-15**

A few months ago, this concert room was called the Triptyque, a great place for live rock'n'roll and indie music concerts. Today, the Social Club hosts parties closer to the techno side of the music world. Nevertheless, you can still observe and interact with the Parisian hipsters: guys with slim jeans, Ray-Bans and mop-tops fill the place, quaffing beers with the utmost cool... Cliché? Absolutely not!

## Truskel
LIVE MUSIC

**2 Rue Feydeau, 2nd • M° Grands-Boulevards**
**www.truskel.com • No cover charge**

It has only taken the Truskel a couple of years to become a fix for rock addicts... This former Irish pub (the front is green!) has both beer (of course) and live DJ music on tap for your enjoyment. And after-hours, some of the greatest rock bands of the time have set up on the stage here (Franz Ferdinand, The Kills!)... Slim pants, hats and old-fashioned glasses are a must to blend in...

My addresses around Opéra and Palais-Royal
_____
_____
_____
_____
_____
_____

# Culture Mix

**W**elcome to the cultural heart of Paris! The Louvre remains the treasure of the city, but under Napoleon III, in the second half of the 19th century, a major urban and architectural overhaul gave the streets the look they have today. Baron Haussmann, the city prefect appointed to re-design the city, ushered in the modernism of the department stores and the Opéra House by replacing narrow medieval streets with wide avenues and boulevards. Modernity discreetly continues to color these historical landmarks, sometimes stirring controversy: the Louvre pyramid, the Buren columns and the fairy-tale Métro entrance designed by Jean-François Othoniel on the Place Colette, in front of the Comédie Française. Travel through time; you're sure to make some amazing discoveries.

## Musée des Arts Décoratifs
DECORATIVE ARTS

**107 Rue de Rivoli, 1st**
**M° Palais-Royal-Musée-du-Louvre**
**www.lesartsdecoratifs.fr • 01 44 55 57 50**
**Admission: €8**
**Tuesday-Friday 11 am-6 pm; weekend 10 am-6 pm;**
**Thursday 11 am-9 pm; closed Monday.**
**Closed January 1st, May 1st, and December 25th**

Lovers of design, furniture, and objects enjoy visiting the Musée des Arts Décoratifs, located in the wing of the Louvre that runs along the Rue de Rivoli. It is a journey through the history of our movable worldly possessions, from the Middle Ages, the Renaissance, the 17th-18th-19th centuries, Art Nouveau, Art Déco to Modern times. You'll be amazed to discover the links between different periods. Clearly, the objects we live with and take for granted tell a story. In the rooms dedicated to toy history, you might even fall back into childhood memories.
The bookshop and design shop (107 Rue de Rivoli) are great places to buy coffee table books you absolutely need or just old-fashioned postcards. If you want to have lunch right on the Tuileries Garden, try "Le Saut du Loup," a trendy restaurant on the ground floor of the museum. For a thrillingly instructive afternoon...

## Cour Carrée
LOUVRE

**1st • M° Louvre-Rivoli**
**www.louvre.fr**
**Daily (except Tuesday) 9 am-**
**6 pm; Wednesday and Friday**
**evening to 10 pm. Closed**
**January 1st, May 1st, November**
**11th, and December 25th**
**Admission: €9; free the first**
**Sunday of every month.**

Be sure to visit the Cour Carrée courtyard at the eastern end of the monument before you go inside. Magnificent and spacious, it's a perfect example of French Renaissance style. The façade is the oldest of the museum (16th century), and offers an illustration of the fundamentals of architecture. Linger for a moment, looking at the details, and soak up the history of this unique monument. From the Cour Carrée, there's an open passage leading to the heart of the museum, where you can get a surprising view of I.M. Pei's pyramid, sitting as if it had always been there.

## Kiosque des Noctambules
MÉTRO STATION

**Place Colette, 1st**
**M° Palais-Royal-Musée-du-Louvre**

The Métropolitain is quintessentially Parisian. In 2000, Paris celebrated the centennial of this wonderful transportation system, considered one of the world's best.

Many stations from that period have been preserved and the typical Art Nouveau signature of their designer, Hector Guimard, is still very visible in the city. For its 100th birthday, the RATP (Transportation Authority of Paris) launched a competition to design a specific Métro station in the heart of Paris, just in front of la Comédie Française. Inspired by the Parisian newspaper stands, French sculptor Jean-Michel Othoniel designed a kiosk bejeweled with 800 glass beads, a magical and colorful way to emerge from the underground labyrinth of Paris and enjoy a night at the theater. The work of art also sparkles in the sunrise, for an after-the-party delight...

# Jardins du Palais-Royal
ROYAL GARDEN AND MODERN SCULPTURE

**Place du Palais-Royal • M° Palais-Royal-Musée-du-Louvre**

Today it's the Ministry of Culture and Communication, but the Palais-Royal used to be the home of Cardinal Richelieu, as well as many aristocrats and blue-bloods from French history. The stately gardens seem like a safe haven nowadays, but this is one of the places where the French Revolution started, and where Parisians began their quest for freedom from monarchy. In 1986, French artist Daniel Buren designed a witty response to the colonnaded galleries, with a sculpture which is both a variation on the theme and an homage to the caryatids, the ladies of stone holding up the building. Another example of "architectural juxtaposition" in the 1st arrondissement: the Ministry's brand-new façade, where a latticed skin created by Francis Solers surrounds the old structure (182 Rue Saint-Honoré, 1st • M° Louvre-Rivoli).

# Le Laboratoire
CONTEMPORARY ART & SCIENCE

**4 Rue du Bouloi, 1st • M° Louvre-Rivoli**
**www.lelaboratoire.org • 01 78 09 49 50 • Admission: €6**
**Friday-Monday 11 am-8 pm. Closed January 1st, May 1st, and December 25th**

With its 14,000 square meters, le Laboratoire is a new kind of cultural place: the idea is to bring together artist/designers and scientists. The experiment, "Artscience," hypothesizes that the connection between different types of personalities, backgrounds and thinking creates a new way of seeing, imagining new forms, searching for possibilities... Industry meets art, poetry reacts to forms and formulas: an interesting visit through new points of view. Tours in English are free and available by request.

# Olympia
PARIS'S OLDEST OPERATING MUSIC HALL

**28 Boulevard des Capucines, 9th • M° Madeleine or Opéra**
**Ticket sales: 0 892 68 33 68**

Are you ready to experience a genuine "nuit parisienne"? Then head to the Olympia, one of Paris's most precious landmarks. It is the city's oldest operating music hall, created in 1888 and totally restored in the 90s to its original beauty. For decades, it has been one of the most coveted venues for the greatest French and international artists, such as Dalida, Jacques Brel, Joséphine Baker... even the Beatles! When entering this hall, you can always feel the thrill of its glamorous past, while staying up to date with the latest in French songsters.

## Palais Garnier
PARIS' HISTORICAL OPERA HOUSE

**Place de l'Opéra, 9th • M° Opéra**
**08 92 89 90 90**
**Daily for tours 10 am-5 pm**

## Opéra Bastille
PARIS' MODERN OPERA HOUSE

**Place de la Bastille, 12th • M° Bastille**
**08 36 69 78 68**
**Opening times vary**

Each of the two opera house symbolizes a different era in architecture, but lovers of classical music, opera and ballet are faithful to both.

The Opéra Garnier is the historical and breathtaking home of highbrow song and dance, the old-fashioned, magical experience of seeing and being seen in Paris. You will feel like wearing white gloves and ordering champagne!

Bastille takes you on a contemporary journey, complete with state-of-the-art acoustics. The show will make you fly through time and music on the first note.

A bit expensive, but what an unforgettable evening!

**Reservations** for the Opéra can be tricky, since shows are expensive and often sold out. We strongly advise that you reserve in advance:

• **On the web** (in French only): www.operadeparis.fr
• **By phone**: 0 892 89 90 90 Monday-Friday, 9 am-6 pm and Saturday morning. From abroad: 33 1 72 29 35 35.
• **On the spot**: The box offices of both theaters are open daily 10:30 am to 6:30 pm, except Sundays and holidays. The Palais Garnier box office is located at the corner of Rues Scribe and Auber. Opéra Bastille box office: 130 Rue de Lyon.

## Opéra Comique
PARIS' POPULAR OPERA HOUSE

**5 Rue Favart, 2nd • M° Richelieu-Drouot**
**www.opera-comique.com**
**08 25 01 01 23**

More discreet than its famous counter-parts Bastille and Garnier, the Opéra Comique historically represents the popular, lightweight vein of Parisian melomania. It dates back to the 18th century, when it was an alternative to the aristocratic venues, and it has never forsaken its character. Its walls now resound with baroque music as well as opera and various forgotten master-pieces, attracting modern crowds.

### Good deals on tickets!

Three ticket booths in Paris offer **half-price tickets** on many shows and plays, for the same day or within the following few days.

• Place de la Madeleine (near the church)

• Place des Ternes (center, between flower shops)

• Montparnasse Train Station (near the Montparnasse tower on the esplanade)

Tuesday-Saturday (12 to 8 pm) and Sundays (12:30 to 4 pm)

# Shopping
# Chic

**S** tart the stroll at Palais-Royal, enter Rue Saint-Honoré, and follow our lead all the way to Place Vendôme, the jewelry district, where the shop windows of the renowned French brands will certainly make your eyes sparkle with dreams of fame and fortune... To keep you from feeling frustrated, we've selected a few nice, affordable addresses.

⭐ **Icon:** Anna Mouglalis, actress

## Astier de Villatte

HOME

**173 Rue Saint-Honoré, 1st**
**M° Palais-Royal-Musée-du-Louvre or Pyramides**
**Monday-Saturday 11 am-7:30 pm**

Enter this store and you will feel like you've just walked into an old cloister, with the exposed stonework and dark gray walls. The inventory of Dutch furniture has been supplemented by some Shaker pieces, and both are interspersed with handmade china, as delicate as lace, full of mystical poetry.
*Dishes (from €45)*

## Let's be snobs!

••• Never, ever consider buying a fragrance elsewhere than the Serge Lutens boutique. The perfumes of France's greatest "nez," a symbol of Palais-Royal chic, are a delight to the senses in every way. Even their names are pure poetry: Rose de Nuit, Tubéreuse Criminelle... Unforgettable.

**Les Salons du Palais-Royal:**
**25 Rue de Valois, 1st**
**M° Palais-Royal-Musée-du-Louvre**

## Vanessa Bruno
FASHION (WOMEN)

**12 Rue de Castiglione, 1st • M° Tuileries or Concorde**
**Monday-Saturday 10:30 am-7:30 pm**

The famous Parisian designer has nestled her designs in a purely poetic ambience. Browse through her ultra-feminine flimsy dresses and tops, caress the soft leather of her bags and shoes, or just stroll under the flowery tree planted in the middle of the shop. Check out "Athé," Vanessa Bruno's affordable brand.
*Dress (around €200)*

••• Quench your thirst at the Colette water bar, choosing from a selection of 70 waters from around the world... Don't reward the fashionistas with a second glance... Colette is Paris's first concept store: over the past ten years, it has been the place to go to browse new trends and hi-tech consumer goods, and also just to hang out, on an afternoon of shopping in the 1st arrondissement. A must-see...
**Colette: 213 Rue Saint-Honoré, 1st • M° Tuileries**
**www.colette.fr**

## Maje
FASHION (WOMEN)

**267 Rue Saint-Honoré, 1st**
**M° Tuileries or Concorde**
**Monday-Saturday 10 am-7 pm**

Maje is like an island of reasonably priced chic in an ocean of high-ticket clothing. And the good news is that it's a great place to find all you need to pass for a chic Parisian. Well-cut basics such as black pants and gray sweaters, oversized belts and leather bags, and even a nice line of jewelry.
*Sweaters (€150)*

## Maria Luisa
FASHION (WOMEN/MEN)

**Ladies' Wear: 7 Rue Rouget-de-Lisle, 1st • 01 47 03 96 15**
**Menswear: 38 Rue du Mont-Thabor, 1st • 01 42 60 89 83**
**Monday-Saturday 10:30 am-7 pm**

This multi-brand specialist scales the highest peaks of fashion, and is a must-see for every pro in the garment trade, whether they wield needle and thread or pen and paper. Not only do you get an eyeful of what's happening, any wardrobe you put together there is bound to be timeless and appropriate in any situation. Maria Luisa dashes in where more angelic buyers fear to tread, merrily wedding opposites. Take a look, at least.
*Dress (from €200)*

## Eres
BATHING SUITS & LINGERIE (WOMEN)
**2 Rue Tronchet, 8th • M° Madeleine**
**Monday-Saturday 10 am-7 pm**

How can wearing only a few centimeters of fabric make one so elegant? Eres is the place to shop for a bathing suit: slinky knits and sublime cuts that last for years. Wherever you vacation, you will feel like you're on the Riviera. And that sensation will endure: almost every Parisian girl I know has had her Eres suit forever! They just never go out of style. Eres also carries a lingerie line.
*Ultimate classic black suit (€200)*

## Repetto
SHOES (WOMEN)
**22 Rue de la Paix, 2nd • M° Opéra**
**Monday-Saturday 9:30 am-7:30 pm**

Entering Repetto is like entering a ballet class: wooden floors, skinny, uptight sales clerks, leotards in every size, pastel tutus, classical music... But the main attraction is clearly the shoes: inspired by ballet slippers, Repettos are today the basic shoe accessory from the Latin Quarter to Pigalle. You've just got to have a pair!
*Repetto pumps (from €140)*

## ➕ Beauty bonanza: get dolled up for free!

While your run-of-the-mill tourist is standing in line at the cash register, the Parisienne is getting made up for free at the Sephora flagship store on the Champs-Élysées, the Galeries Lafayette, or Printemps de la Beauté. Of course, the cosmeticians work fast – it takes them less than ten minutes to freshen up your face, apply the war paint, or offer a free skin or hair diagnosis. The pitch will include advice, a little card with your personal beauty prescription, and some sort of incentive to purchase the cosmetics on offer. However, you needn't feel obligated to haul out your wallet – it's your second time around!

• Galeries Lafayette, 40 Boulevard Haussmann, 9th. M° Chaussée-d'Antin-La Fayette
• Printemps Haussmann, 64 Boulevard Haussmann, 9th. M° Havre-Caumartin
Both stores are open Monday-Saturday 9:35 am-8 pm (10 pm Thursday)
• Also available at the Sephora store on the Champs-Élysées:
70-72 Avenue des Champs-Élysées, 8th. M° George-V. Daily 10 am-12 am

Les Grands Boulevards
Yves Montand

« J'aime flâner sur les Grands
Boulevards
Y a tant de choses, tant de choses,
tant de choses à voir.
On n'a qu'à choisir au hasard
On s'fait des ampoules
A zigzaguer parmi la foule... »

# 2.
# Bastille,
# Marais
# and Châtelet

This area is the gateway to the east side of Paris, where there's a lot going on!
Bastille is the young, lively area north and south of the Rue du Faubourg Saint-Antoine.
It's a great destination for trendy DJ bars and boheme clothing. The Marais neighborhood is one of the best preserved in Paris, with its 17th-century architecture and fascinating history. It also bears the distinction of being the center of both the Ashkenazi Jewish and gay communities, guaranteeing great food and shopping...
Châtelet is a public transportation hub and a main shopping destination in the center of Paris, from the edge of the Seine to Les Halles, once the all-night wholesale food market.

# Parisians'
## Secret
# Eateries

## Bastille

### La Gazzetta

WORLD ◆◆◆

**29 Rue de Cotte, 12th • M° Ledru-Rollin**
**www.lagazzetta.fr • 01 43 47 47 05**
**Tuesday-Saturday 11:30 am-3 pm and 6:30 pm-1 am**

A fine bistro featuring cuisine created by a sexy Swedish chef... The decoration is ultra-simple, placing the focus on the customers and the food... Start with a classic margarita pizza, progress to a potted shoulder of lamb with honey, and top it off with a vanilla-pear soufflé...

### Pause Café

FRENCH LUNCH ◆

**41 Rue de Charonne, 11th • M° Ledru-Rollin or Bastille**
**01 48 06 80 33**
**Daily 10 am-3:30 pm and 7:30 pm-12 am**
**Non-stop Saturdays 12 pm-12 am**

Take a break from browsing the boutiques and galleries on the charming Rue de Charonne, and enjoy the hipster crowd and low-priced menu. From the broad, sunny terrace, you can admire the neighborhood's beautiful people, as you fill up on energy from simple, tasty pasta dishes, cheddar and spinach quiche. The main course might be lamb, with ginger-cookie rice pudding for dessert. Scrumptious and convenient.

### Let's be snobs

Have a simple Sunday morning for once: buy your produce at the **Marché d'Aligre** and eat oysters off one of the barrels standing out in front of the Baron Bouge, a wine bar where you can also fill empty bottles with your favorite vintage, for the week.

**Place d'Aligre, 12th • M° Ledru-Rollin**
**Every morning except on Mondays**
**Baron Bouge:**
**1 Rue Théophile-Roussel, 12th**
**M° Ledru-Rollin • 01 43 43 14 32**

## Unico
ARGENTINA ◆◆

**15 Rue Paul-Bert, 11th • M° Faidherbe-Chaligny**
**www.resto-unico.com • 01 43 67 68 08 (reservations)**
**Tuesday-Saturday 12:30-2:30 pm and 8-10 pm**

A place for meat lovers, created by two pals from Argentina, a land rightly famed for its beef. The converted butcher shop has kept the old-Paris mood alive, with a touch of 1970s French government office to charm your inner bureaucrat. Claude Sautet could have eaten here with Yves Montand and Romy Schneider (may they rest in peace).
The team is friendly, and always ready to kid around. Don't be surprised if you get chummy with the people who are waiting for your table.

## Chez Paul
FRENCH ◆◆

**13 Rue de Charonne, 11th**
**M° Ledru-Rollin or Bastille**
**01 47 00 34 57**
**Monday-Sunday 12-2:30 pm and 7:15 pm-12:30 am**

Amidst the frenzy of bars and clubs around the Bastille, you might long for some peace and quiet, so head to this quaint restaurant with definite character. Created in 1900, the place has not changed a bit: red-and-white-checkered tablecloths, old wood, darkened mirrors and a cushy bourgeois ambience (but beware, it is often crowded!) Expect traditional plates of foie gras or pot au feu.

## La Mansouria
MOROCCAN ◆◆

**11 Rue Faidherbe, 11th • M° Faidherbe-Chaligny**
**01 43 71 00 16**
**Monday-Saturday 7-11 pm; Wednesday-Sunday 12-2 pm**

Leave Paris for a few hours and head to Morocco! La Mansouria welcomes every hungry soul in a typical Moroccan ambience with delicious Oriental food: a choice of couscous, pastillas, and tajines, topped off with mint tea and gooey honey pastries.

## Marais and Châtelet

### L'As du Falafel
JEWISH SNACK ◆

**34 Rue des Rosiers, 4th • M° Saint-Paul**
**01 48 87 63 60**
**Daily (except Saturdays) 12 pm-12 am; Friday 12-5 pm**

You have to visit the Rue des Rosiers, a unique Marais street which is the historical hub of the Parisian Jewish community... Gefilte fish has given way to falafel worthy of Tel Aviv... Crammed with eggplant, cabbage, pickles, and cucumbers in addition to the fried chick-pea balls, the sandwiches have a become a classic of the area. If you opt for trimmings like the spicy harissa sauce, you may shout out Mazel Tov! The faint-hearted will abstain.

### ✚ Sweet delights

Warning: irresistible goodies. Exceptions Gourmandes is a shop which just opened to showcase the wizardry of pastry chef Philippe Conticini. The tiny, ultra-discreet treasure trove is bound to make an addict out of you. The innovative sweets include a lollipop combination of milk chocolate and orange, or a melt-in-your-mouth sand cookie made with the finest Isigny butter from Normandy. The tender caramels are flavored with real coffee, and until you've experienced guimauve, you haven't really tasted marshmallow.

**Exceptions Gourmandes:**
**4 Place du Marché Sainte-Catherine, 4th**
**M° Saint-Paul • 01 42 77 16 50**
**Tuesday-Sunday 12-7 pm**

### Le Loir dans la Théière
BRUNCH & TEA TIME ◆

**3 Rue des Rosiers, 4th • M° Saint-Paul • 01 42 72 90 61**
**Daily 9:30 am-9:30 pm**

People feel so good in this charming restaurant that the owners have had to put a ban on laptops, to ensure that their patrons don't just sit there all day! Old wooden tables and cosily worn leather armchairs make you feel right at home. Have a simple lunch (quiches or veggie tarts around €8), but leave room for dessert: their pies and cakes are famous all over Paris, especially the "tarte au citron" with the huge meringue topping (around €5). We'll say no more...

## Chez Omar
MOROCCAN ◆

**47 Rue de Bretagne, 3rd • M° Filles-du-Calvaire • 01 42 72 36 26**
**Daily 12-2:30 pm and 7-11:30 pm; closed Sunday**

If you're wondering how traditional Moroccan cuisine would taste in a no less traditional French bistro setting, the answer is here. Expect to find a good selection of classic platters such as couscous and tagines (lamb or chicken stews spiced with cinnamon and cumin) and a fabulously rich and yummy North African dessert selection dripping with honey. This place is always packed and is a Marais institution: Beautiful people and your average VIP eat here to be seen and check out the other guests. Another Parisian ritual!

**+**Let's be snobs!

Find any excuse to head to the **Enfants Rouges market**, and eat Japanese food made from scratch at Taeko.

**Marché des Enfants-Rouges:**
**39 Rue de Bretagne, 3rd**
**M° Filles-du-Calvaire**
**Tuesday-Sunday**
**8:30 am-1 pm and 4-7 pm.**

## Thaï Spices
THAÏ ◆ ◆ ◆

**7 Rue de l'Ave-Maria, 4th • M° Saint-Paul**
**01 42 78 65 49**
**Daily 12-3 pm and 7:30-10:30 pm; closed for lunch**
**on weekends**

Located in the Saint-Paul area, Thaï Spices is perfect for a romantic dinner. An intimate setting, fine food, discreet waiters and patrons... just relax, hold hands and enjoy the wonderful dishes the talented chef concocts with fine ingredients imported from Thailand. Our fave: thin slices of grilled beef basking in green curry, served with thaï rice pasta, and the chocolate nem for dessert. Mmmmm...

# Le Trésor
ITALIAN ♦♦
**7 Rue du Trésor, 3rd • M° Saint-Paul**
**01 42 71 35 17**
**Daily 9:30-2 am**

In a quiet dead-end street, Le Trésor is a well-known meeting place in the Marais and the right spot to enjoy Italian food under the trees, far from the hectic Rue de Rivoli. Not in the mood for pasta? Try the minestrone, served lukewarm, the swordfish "alla puttanesca" (with capers, tomatoes, olives), or the Veal Picata. Italian treasures...

# Mai Thai
THAÏ ♦♦
**24 bis Rue Saint-Gilles, 3rd • M° Chemin-Vert**
**www.maithai.fr • 01 42 72 18 77**
**Monday-Friday 11 am-2:30 pm and daily 6-10:30 pm**

A precious address for many reasons: its location in the heart of the Marais, its calm terrace, its non-kitsch ambience and, of course, its delicious Siam food. Just imagine: fresh papaya salad, mountain rice cooked in coconut milk, red curry duck... The chef is aware that some like it mild, so if you're one of them, be sure to let the waiter know...

# Les Bougresses
FRENCH ♦
**6 Rue de Jarente, 4th • M° Saint-Paul**
**01 48 87 71 21**
**Tuesday-Sunday 6-11:30 pm**

Why do people always come back here? It could be the fabulous location on the place du Marché-Sainte-Catherine, or the freshly made, reasonably-priced dishes, or the excitement of the wine list... We've investigated the matter, and it seems that what attracts people is the way they're greeted with a smile... It feels like coming home.

My addresses around Marais and Châtelet

## Chez Julien
FRENCH ◆◆

**1 Rue du Pont-Louis-Philippe, 4th • M° Pont-Marie**
**01 42 78 31 64**
**Monday-Saturday 12-3 pm and 7-11 pm**

Chic and charming address located right on the Seine facing Île Saint-Louis, on the picturesque Rue des Barres, a medieval-feeling street behind Saint-Gervais church. Its very French menu and bouquets of white roses give the place a touch of 19th-romanticism... Prepare for some virtuoso turns on French cuisine classics, like the pot au feu of foie gras de canard, a magnificent sole, or the down-home boudin noir. It's so goooooooooood!

## Le Louchebem
FRENCH ◆◆

**31 Rue Berger, 1st • M° Châtelet or Les Halles**
**www.le-louchebem.fr • 01 42 33 12 99**
**Monday-Saturday 12-2:30 pm and 7-11:30 pm**

This restaurant, a relic of the golden age of Les Halles as "the belly of Paris," the city's wholesale food market, is located' in an old butcher's shop. "Louchebem" means "butcher" in the slang that was tossed around by the workers, and a meal at Louchebem is a journey into the world of meat and its iconography Any piece of the cow or the chicken is on the menu, and when it hits your plate, it's luscious. Vegetarians, go home!

## Le Trumilou
FRENCH ◆

**84 Quai de l'Hôtel-de-Ville, 4th • M° Hôtel-de-Ville**
**Tel: 01 42 77 63 98**
**Daily 12-3 pm and 7-11 pm**

A quiet family bistro in the heart of Paris offering traditional French fare such as the tender mijoté de canard aux pruneaux (duck with prunes) or the andouillette, a roasted sausage served with homemade French fries and mustard sauce. The Trumilou is prized by Parisians for its terrace and relaxed provincial touch.

# The Night Time is the Right Time

This area is 'all about bars in a young, friendly, multicultural ambience in the Bastille neighborhood, around the Rue de Charonne, Rue Keller and the Rue des Taillandiers. Don't waste your time with the Rue de Lappe or the Rue de la Roquette, which mainly attract tourists, not near-Parisians like you. The "It Streets" of the moment are Rue Jean-Pierre-Timbaud, Rue Vieille-du-Temple, and Rue Charlot in upper Marais (north of the center, heading towards République).

## Bastille

### Motel
DRINKS & LIVE MUSIC

**8 Passage Josset, 11th • M° Ledru-Rollin**
**01 58 30 88 52 • Tuesday-Sunday 6 pm-1:45 am**

Fresh, exciting, joyous, and fun! The Motel is a sensational invention, a great place to hang out and have a drink, if you don't mind the crowd. This neighborhood is packed with happening bars, but the Motel has soul: friendly staff, cheap beer, DJ mixing, and light dancing. The circular bar makes it easy to spot new people and hook up.

### Planète Mars
DRINKS

**21 Rue Keller, 11th • M° Ledru-Rollin**
**01 43 14 24 44 • Monday-Saturday 6:30 pm-2 am**

Pint-sized' Planète Mars is often jammed "bumper to bumper". There's no seating, but the music is good, and the owner is a nice guy. Ask him for his special cocktail with vodka... A delight.

### La Mécanique Ondulatoire
DRINKS

**8 Passage Thieré, 11th • M° Ledru-Rollin**
**www.lamecond.com • Monday-Saturday 6 pm-2 am**

An up-and-coming nightspot, La Mécanique Ondulatoire offers two different atmospheres: a low-key bar and concert hall in the basement, and an exhibition space on the ground floor. All kinds of music are represented here, from rock'n'roll, to funk and DJ mixes (the must of this area).

## La Scène Bastille
DRINKS, LIVE MUSIC & DANCING

**2 bis Rue des Taillandiers, 11th • M° Ledru-Rollin**
**www.la-scene.com**

La Scène is a small concert hall hosting new, start-up bands. The businesslike, no-frills venue is known as a proving ground. You can help launch a rising star! Theme nights like In Funk We Trust and the Apéro du Jeudi are scheduled regularly. There's no problem getting in, but you'll have trouble getting out!

## Marais and Châtelet

## Le Pick-Clops
DRINKS

**16 Rue Vieille-du-Temple, 4th • M° Hôtel-de-Ville or Saint-Paul**
**01 40 29 02 18 • Daily 7 am-2 am**

This is your beloved "corner bar," the perfect place to meet friends for a drink. As soon as you see the long zinc counter, you'll feel like a beer from the tap. The atmosphere is upbeat, a shrine to the early years of rock'n'roll. Formica, vinyl, and cardboard rule, with wild colors, imagined in a Parisian way... The crowd is young and neighborly, far away from the loud bars of the area.

## Le Petit Fer à Cheval
DRINKS

**30 Rue Vieille-du-Temple, 4th • M° Saint-Paul or Hôtel-de-Ville**
**01 42 72 47 47 • Daily 8-2 am**

Although this postage-stamp-sized bar hasn't changed a whit since 1903, the horseshoe-shaped zinc counter and the benches, from old Métro coaches, have discovered the fountain of youth. The place is always packed with the clientele now fashionable in the neighborhood. Old pots make the best soup, as they say! Nevertheless, if there's no room for more merrymakers, head for La Chaise au Plafond (10 Rue du Trésor) or Pick-Clops.

## La Perle
DRINKS

**78 Rue Vieille-du-Temple, 3rd • M° Saint-Paul**
**01 42 72 69 93 • Daily 6 pm-2 am**

La Perle is an institution: at the crossroads of the two Marais (yes, there are two! The classical 4th-arrondissement one and the boboish 3rd arrondissement Upper Marais), this bar is the throbbing heart of the area. The regulars have their habits, but new faces are welcome... You may end up on the sidewalk, but hey, you're in Paris! If you're lucky, you'll glimpse some of France's hottest actors popping in for coffee.

## Duc des Lombards
DRINKS & LIVE MUSIC

**42 Rue des Lombards, 1st**
**M° Châtelet**
**www.ducdeslombards.com**
**01 42 33 22 88**

This is one of the few jazz institutions of Paris: recently renovated, the place screams design and lounge, a radical departure from the dark, discreet atmosphere you would expect... But the result is classy: the space offers wonderful visibility and warmth, where wood meets purple and cream colors. The proximity of the stage is practically a statement of the new owners' values: when you love jazz, you have to snuggle up close! Reservations recommended.

**+**

## Bucolic urban bliss!
The area known as the **Carreau du Temple** (between Rues Eugène-Spuller and Dupetit-Thouars, M° Temple or République), named for the mysterious, medieval Knights Templar, whose headquarters stood here until Napoleon had them torn down in 1808, became a covered marketplace in 1863. Today, cafe and restaurant terraces have taken root all around, and in the summertime, the tables are mobbed with all the trendiest young graphic artists, videographers, and other creators. Minimal automobile traffic, maximal sun, good cooking, and an impeccable allure: the Carreau is where it's at!

## Sunset/Sunside
DRINKS & LIVE MUSIC

**60 Rue des Lombards, 1st • M° Châtelet**
**www.sunset-sunside.com • 01 40 26 46 60**

This is the other authentic jazz venue of the area. In an old, stone-lined cellar, great musicians enjoy intimate moments with their public. It feels like New York...!

# Culture Mix

**D**efinitely contemporary! From the Centre Pompidou, our thirty-year-young National Museum of Modern Art, Renzo Piano's original (and controversial) architectural achievement, to the up-and-coming exhibition spaces further east, the area is a must for lovers of 20th-century art. Check new trends in photography at the Maison Européenne de la Photographie and soak up Parisian history at the Salle Saint-Jean of the Hôtel-de-Ville.

## Bastille

### La Maison Rouge
CONTEMPORARY ART EXHIBITIONS

**10 Boulevard de la Bastille, 12th • M° Bastille or Quai-de-la-Rapée**
**www.lamaisonrouge.org • 01 40 01 08 81 • Admission: €6.50**
**Wednesday-Sunday 11 am-7 pm; Thursday until 9 pm**
**Closed January 1st, May 1st, and December 25th**

The privately-funded Maison Rouge is a showcase for new art, whatever the form: independent curators are invited to organize exhibits four to six times per year. It's a wonderful way to keep up with the artistic zeitgeist, and it's rarely crowded, so it's relaxing. Recharge your batteries and rest your feet at the museum café, or check out the restaurant. This red-themed loft feels like New York's Chelsea or London's Soho, a vibe that's rare in the French capital, so don't miss it. Thumbs up for the layout and scenography.

### Promenade Plantée (ou Coulée verte)
4 KM WALK FROM BASTILLE TO VINCENNES

**Starting M° Bastille • Sunrise to sunset**

In the late 1980s, this promenade was built on the rail line which ran from Bastille to Vincennes in the 19th century. You start by overlooking the 12th arrondissement from the pleasantly landscaped elevated platform, 15 meters above the streets. It's an excellent outing on a sunny day, but for the safety of babies in carriages, skates and bikes are confined to the broad sidewalks of Avenue Daumesnil below. East of the Jardin de Reuilly, though, everyone can roll merrily along at ground level. The car-less peace and quiet make this promenade a must.

# Marais and Châtelet

## Maison Européenne de la Photographie
PHOTO

**5/7 Rue de Fourcy, 4th • M° Saint-Paul or Pont-Marie**
**www.mep-fr.org • 01 44 78 75 00 90 • Admission: €6**
**Wednesday-Sunday 11 am-8 pm**
**Closed January 1st, May 1st, July 14th, August 15th, and December 25th**

Paris has always been a hotspot for innovation in photography, and the city boasts a number of museums and galleries dedicated to this powerful art form. The "MEP," as Parisians refer to it, is located in the heart of the Marais, in a peaceful eighteenth-century "hôtel particulier" typical of the neighborhood. The permanent collection houses work dating from the 1950s to today, and a prestigious roster of contemporary photographers exhibits there.

## Centre Culturel Suédois
CULTURAL CENTER & CAFÉ

**11 Rue Payenne, 3rd • M° Saint-Paul**
**www.si.se • 01 44 78 80 20**
**Tuesday-Saturday 10 am-1 pm and 2-5.30 pm**

Located in the Hôtel de Marle, an architectural treasure, the Swedish Cultural Center gives you an opportunity to hobnob with the country's culturati at art and design shows, film screenings, and lectures. The courtyard café is sheer paradise in beautiful weather.

## Free sights to see!

Native Parisians are aware that admission to the permanent collections of the museums administered by the City of Paris is free, every day of the week. And the municipal museums certainly have plenty to boast about: they include the usual repositories of art and history, the private homes of great 19th-century novelists, and artists' studios. We award top prize for charm to the Musée de la Vie Romantique, with a very special mention going to Musée Cernuschi (Chinese art) and the Petit Palais.

Check out the following: Musée d'Art Moderne, Maison de Balzac, Musée Carnavalet, Musée Cognacq-Jay, Musée Galliera, Petit Palais, Musée Zadkine, Maison de Victor Hugo, Musée de la Vie Romantique, Atelier Brancusi, Atelier d'Antoine Bourdelle (see www.paris.fr for addresses).

**Scattered around the city, they are all open Tuesday-Sunday 10 am-6 pm**

## Musée de la Chasse et de la Nature
HUNTING

**62 Rue des Archives, 3rd • M° Hôtel-de-Ville**
**www.chassenature.org • 01 53 01 92 40**
**Tuesday-Sunday 11 am-6 pm**

This surprising and original collection, housed in a remarkable mansion, focuses on the strong link between man and Nature. It is filled with poetry and love, a paean to the natural world. There are hunting instruments from all ages,

trophies, paintings, and sculpture. The museum regularly welcomes contemporary artists, which brings a touch of modernity to the place.

## ✛ Art Adventure: The Marais gallery jaunt

Get a gander of the artists in the vanguard of the international scene by wandering around the neighborhood, checking out the galleries. They are open Tuesday through Saturday, and admission is free, of course. Our recommendations may save you some time:

For more information on galleries and the world of contemporary art in Paris, check
**www.paris-art.com**

### Emmanuel Perrotin

**76 Rue de Turenne, 3rd • M° Saint-Sébastien Froissart**
**www.galerieperrotin.com**

Everybody knows Emmanuel Perrotin, one of Paris's hot gallery owners... His selection of artists features a great diversity of styles: Sophie Calle, Takashi Murakami, Maurizio Cattelan, Xavier Veilhan... Quite pop and trendy. Emmanuel Perrotin owns also a gallery in Miami... How chic is that?!

### Almine Rech

**19 Rue de Saintonge, 3rd • M° Filles-du -Calvaire**
**www.galeriealminerech.com**

Almine Rech presents contemporary artists such as James Turrel, Hedi Slimane, Nobuyoshi Araki...An absolute must for photo lovers.

## Musée Carnavalet
PARIS HISTORY

**23 Rue de Sévigné, 3rd. M° Saint-Paul or Chemin-Vert**
**www.carnavalet.paris.fr • 01 44 59 58 58**
**Tuesday-Sunday 10 am-6 pm**
**Free admission to the permanent collection; admission to temporary exhibits**
**varies.**

The 140 rooms of the Musée Carnavalet house the city's memory, from its rise in the Middle Ages through the upheavals of the Revolution and beyond. Nothing about this history museum is ho-hum – quite the contrary. The visitor strolls through the huge mansion, deciphering the city's past as represented in paintings, maps, old shop signs, prints, photographs, historical scenes, and such varied mementoes as the red liberty cap of a sans-culotte or articles that once belonged to Voltaire and Rousseau. One of the museum's big plusses is the reconstruction of entire settings, like Marcel Proust's bedroom or the aristocratic reception room of an 18th-century townhouse.

## Marian Goodman
**79 Rue du Temple, 3rd • M° Rambuteau**
**www.mariangoodman.com**

Manhattan art maven Marian Goodman has installed her Paris branch in an impressive townhouse. She exhibits work by Christian Boltanski, Annette Messager, Tony Cragg, and British artist/filmmaker Steve McQueen.

## Espace Claude Berri
**4 Passage Sainte-Avoye, 3rd • M° Rambuteau**
**www.espace-claudeberri.com**

When you're a great French film director/producer and an enlightened contemporary art-lover, your brand-new gallery is well worth a visit.

## Le Passage de Retz
**9 Rue Charlot, 3rd • M° Filles-du-Calvaire**
**www.passagederetz.com**

Since 1994, this 750-square-meter space between garden and courtyard in the 17th-century palace of the Cardinal of Retz (he was actually a Florentine nobleman) has hosted temporary shows curated by a variety of graphic artists, industrial designers, architects, fashion designers, and even philosophers and writers. The eclectic nature of the programming is one of the gallery's most interesting features.

## Centre Pompidou
ART, DESIGN & CINEMA

**Place Georges-Pompidou, 4th • M° Rambuteau**
**www.centrepompidou.fr • 01 44 78 12 33 • Daily (except Tuesday), 11 am-10 pm.**
**Closed May 1st • Admission: €10 (Museum & temporary exhibits)**

The Centre Pompidou focuses on 20th- and 21st-century creations by Matisse, Picasso, and Marcel Duchamp to recent works by Louise Bourgeois, Pierre Huygues, Bruce Naumann, Christian Boltanski, or Sophie Calle. The museum regularly rotates its collection, composed of more than 59,000 works. A place to encounter and connect with culture, it also offers a library, a bookshop, a design boutique, a movie theater, and the acclaimed "Georges" restaurant located on the top floor of the museum. The eatery boasts one of the greatest views of the city, hovering just above its incomparable rooftops... The unique modern architecture, by Renzo Piano and Richard Rogers, a 1977

take on factory design located in the heart of traditional Paris, earned the Centre the nickname "raffinerie de la culture". The vast plaza is one of the most popular meeting points in the center of Paris, and sculptor Constantin Brancusi's studio has been relocated to one corner of it. Brancusi, born in Romania, was one of the inventors of modernist sculpture and a contemporary of Braque and Picasso. Admission to his atelier is free.

## Hôtel de Ville de Paris, Salle Saint-Jean
EXHIBITIONS

**5 Rue de Lobau, 4th • M° Hôtel-de-Ville**
**Monday-Saturday 10 am-7 pm • Admission: Free**

The Salle Saint-Jean gallery inside the Hotel de Ville, Paris's town hall, accessible by the Rue de Rivoli entrance, is the place to discover artists who have a personal history with the city. Through photography or documents, you can experience their symbiotic relationship with Paris: a very special way to visit the city!

My addresses around Marais and Châtelet
_____
_____
_____
_____

# Shopping
# Trendy

**R**eputedly the epicenter of Paris hipsterism, if such an ever-shifting concept can ever be pinpointed on the space-time continuum. In any case, this is where the cutting-edge designers of bobo-wear, like Isabel Marant, have opened their shops, along with highly eccentric multi-brand shops catering to niche markets like skateboarders (and wannabees, of course) and budding designers attempting a breakthrough into the ruthless world of fashion. Catch them while they're just a flash in the pan. In other words, the neighborhood between the Rue des Francs-Bourgeois (where all the shops are open on Sunday), Rues Keller and de Charonne east of the Bastille, and, of course, Rue Vieille-du-Temple, is the shopping addict's paradise. Go right ahead and chat with the staff in the little boutiques - the person behind the counter is often the designer.

⭐ **Icon:** Camille, po-mo chanteuse and sound explorer

## Bastille

### Loulou Addict
OBJECTS & DESIGN

**25 Rue Keller, 11th • M° Bastille or Voltaire • Tuesday-Saturday 11 am-7:30 pm**

This is the address for gift ideas with a sensible touch. A universe recalling childhood memories, filled with printed fabrics, colored plastic glasses, and poetic gift cards. Japanese and Scandinavian inspirations are blended in Loulou Addict's selection: Linum, Greenage Copenhagen, and Rice are among the brands that give the shop its eco-friendly flavor.
*RICE Basket (€49) / "La Fée Belle" Stickers (€17) / Hand-painted paper garland (€27)*

### Anne Willi
FASHION (WOMEN/CHILDREN)

**13 Rue Keller, 11th • M° Bastille or Voltaire**
**Tuesday-Saturday 11:30 am-8 pm; Monday 2-6 pm**

The artsy craftsmanship exuded by Anne Willi's boutique probably seeps in from her workshop next door. The natural roughness of her fabrics combines perfectly with the simplicity of the shapes. The casual clothing in forest greens, aubergines, and earthy browns will immediately convince you to embrace the natural look and run off to the country, like any Parisian worth his salt. All of this cuddled in warm sweaters for a perfect bohemian look.
*Dress (€198) / Necklace (€55)*

## Marci N'oum
FASHION (WOMEN/CHILDREN)

**1 Rue Keller, 11th • M° Bastille or Voltaire**
**Tuesday-Saturday 11:30 am-7 pm; Monday 2-7 pm**

If you're desperately searching for the perfect bag at a reasonable price, you may find it at Marci N'oum. This boutique offers a small but interesting selection of handbags: soft forms and pastel colors will definitely give a boost to whatever you're wearing. Get ready for a love affair!
*Necklace (€70-90) / Earrings (€38) / Handbag (€150)*

## French Trotters
FASHION (WOMEN/MEN)

**30 Rue de Charonne, 11th • M° Bastille or Voltaire**
**Monday-Saturday 11 am-7:30 pm**

FrenchTrotters is the arty address of Rue de Charonne: a mix of art (exhibitions of illustrators, photographers) and exclusive brands (Les Prairies de Paris, Gaspard Yurkievich)... It's comparable in feel to Colette, with a concept-store display. Okay, it's a bit pricey, but isn't it always good to visit places that inspire you?
*Maloles ballerinas (€205) / Gloves Maison Favre (€100) / Parka for men (€270)*

## Sessùn
FASHION (WOMEN)

**30 Rue de Charonne, 11th • M° Bastille or Voltaire**
**Monday-Saturday 11 am-7 pm**

Any brand based in Marseille HAS TO be interesting! Sessùn presents a very original wardrobe inspired by urban culture and worldwide fashion: you can't really tell where it comes from... It's Japanese in the modern shapes and cuts, Scandinavian in the printed fabrics and the architectural look of the shop, and definitely French for the charming details...
*Tunic dress (€103) / Parka (€185)*

## Delphine Pariente
FASHION (WOMEN)

**30 Rue de Charonne, 11th • M° Ledru-Rollin**
**Monday-Saturday 11:30 am-7 pm**

A small shop hosting great stuff: clothes, yes, and jewelry, yeah! Delphine Pariente creates necklaces, bracelets, and grigri amulets with charming vintage elements.
*Sweater (€100) / Dress (€140)*

# Isabel Marant
FASHION (WOMEN/CHILDREN)

**16 Rue de Charonne, 11th • M° Bastille or Voltaire**
**Monday-Saturday 10:30 am-7:30 pm**

Isabel Marant is one of France's most talented designers. She has won her place in the fashion world as well as in fashionistas' hearts, fair and square! A symbol of the bohemian east-side-of-Paris look, her fashion is a poetic, folky, and melancholic view of what she herself would like to wear every day. Dresses in simple fabrics, second-skin sweaters you'll want to sleep in, old school jewelry: our dream wardrobe... Isabel also makes Etoile, a more affordable brand.
*Dress (€230) / Sweater (€225) / Necklace (€60-120)*

# Almost Famous
FASHION (WOMEN)

**33 Rue de Charonne, 11th • M° Ledru-Rollin**
**Tuesday-Saturday 10 am-7 pm**

A selection of the best fashion in the city! No Dior or Saint-Laurent, but edgy clothes selected by definite trendsetters.
*Pants (€150) / Sweater (€120)*

# Klok
MATERNITY WEAR

**27 Rue Keller, 11th • M° Ledru-Rollin**
**Tuesday-Saturday 11 am-2 pm and 2:30-7 pm**

It's not impossible to find attractive, affordable maternity clothes in Paris. Check out Klok, which means "pregnant" in slang... Lots of fun for the shopper who's expecting. They also have a selection of baby clothes and soft homemade toys.
*Dress (€160)*

# Galerie Patrick Seguin
FURNITURE BY JEAN PROUVÉ AND CO

**5 Rue des Taillandiers, 11th • M° Ledru-Rollin**
**www.patrickseguin.com**
**Tuesday-Saturday 10am-7pm**

A moment of design serenity at Galerie Jousse Seguin is a must while you shop around Rue de Charonne. If you don't know Jean Prouvé, beware! You may fall in love. A great French industrial designer, he imagined furniture mixing wood and steel in a minimalist yet graphic way that you'll have absolutely no trouble seeing in your apartment.

# Marais and Châtelet

## Brontibay
BAGS

**6 Rue de Sévigné, 4th • M° Saint-Paul**
**Monday-Saturday 11 am-8 pm; Sunday 1:30-7:30 pm**

As accessories, these bags will be the icing on your outfit's cake! Bright and colorful, the Brontibay collection is exciting. The universe is a bit pop, with a large selection of sizes, styles, and forms, but always with a juicy shine. The only hitch is that you'll have trouble making up your mind... It's the kingdom of pocket bags (pochette) and shoulder straps, featuring a variety of sizes for each design...
*Small bag (€95) / Pocket bag (€39)*

## Muji
FASHION & HOME

**47 Rue des Francs-Bourgeois, 4th • M° Saint-Paul**
**Monday-Friday 10 am-7:30 pm; Saturday 10 am-8 pm**

This is the Japanese brand with no name. That is the actual translation of MUJI, a "no logo" fashion that keeps it hush-hush. The ultimate in inconspic-uous elegance! Nevertheless, a style was born. The clothes have a city look that you can skew by wearing Japanese toe socks. The lifestyle department is an exercise in simplicity and minimalism, with a large selection of useful and desirable accessories for the office, kitchen, and bathroom.
*Men's shoes (€59) / Socks (€3.50) / Pen (€1.25)*

## Autour du Monde
FASHION & HOME

**8 Rue des Francs-Bourgeois, 4th • M° Saint-Paul**
**Monday-Saturday 11 am-7 pm; Sunday 1:30-7 pm**

A dual-purpose shop where you can dress up both your home and yourself. Fashion is represented by Bensimon, the classic French sportswear brand, famous for its faded tones and popular tennis shoes. Bensimon selects objects and furniture that are a mix of design, ethnic influences, and craft: humor is the heart of this boutique, a great spot to feel the trends in lifestyle...
*Candlestick (€20) / Toiletry bag (€24) / Cotton dress (€95) / Tennis shoes (€24)*

## Erotokritos
FASHION (WOMEN/MEN)

**99 Rue Vieille-du-Temple, 3rd • M° Saint-Paul**
**Tuesday-Saturday 11 am-7:30 pm; Sunday 2-7:30 pm; Monday 1-7:30 pm**

Erotokritos is a Greek-Cypriot designer who has captured Parisians' hearts: the location of his Marais boutique just behind the Musée Picasso may not be a coincidence... His fashion roughs up the classics with a glittery edge, and his handmade, to-die-for buttons are pure magic: they change everything. It's like disco music over the PA system in a prep school classroom...!
*Men's T-shirt (€95) / Shoes (€215)*

## nocollection
FASHION (WOMEN/CHILDREN)

**96 Rue Vieille-du-Temple, 3rd • M° Saint-Paul**
**Tuesday-Saturday 11 am-7:30 pm**
**Monday 2-7:30 pm**

The atmosphere is pearl grey; the clothes in solid tones of dusty pink, plum, and pale green. Wonderfully-cut dresses will wake up the woman in you... It's classic that never dies, but with a modern touch in details and color. Very warm and charming, so easy to accessorize.
*Dress (€140-200)*

## Galerie Simone
FASHION (WOMEN/ACCESSORIES)

**124 Rue Vieille-du-Temple, 3rd • M° Saint-Paul**
**Tuesday-Saturday 12-7 pm**

Galerie Simone offers an out-of-the-blue selection, showing designers from all over the world – Korea, Japan, Romania, and Poland, to name a few. It's a bit overwhelming at first, but once you take the time to sort things out, you'll love it. The feeling is very "work-in-progress," a bit like today's fashion. The handmade jewelry is one of the best parts of the visit!
*Silver ring (€47) / Bracelet (€35) / Dress (€235)*

## Abu Dhabi Bazaar
FASHION (WOMEN)

**10 Rue des Francs-Bourgeois, 3rd • M° Saint-Paul
Tuesday-Saturday 10:30 am-7:15 pm; Sunday and
Monday 2-7:15 pm**

All the designers you need to feel relaxed and
receptive; Zen, right? Repetto, Isabel Marant, Bali
Barret, Iro, BA&SH, Sandro, etc. This famous Rue
des Francs-Bourgeois venue will familiarize you
with the season's trends developed by your
favorite brands.
*Shirt (from €50) / Dress (around €100)*

## CSAO
FASHION & OBJECTS

**9 Rue Elzévir, 3rd • M° Saint-Paul
Monday-Saturday 11 am-1 pm
and 2-7 pm**

A showcase for African arts &
crafts, with clothing and accessories straight from the talented
designers and recyclers of
Senegal and Western Africa.
Gifts to amaze the folks back
home.
*Objects from €5*

## PLAGG
FASHION FROM SCANDINAVIA (WOMEN)

**41 Rue Charlot, 3rd • M° Filles-du-Calvaire
Tuesday-Saturday 11 am-8 pm; Sunday 12-8 pm**

This is the place to discover the brilliant new
Danish, Norwegian, and Swedish designers, who
really know how to dress a girl for winter weather.
The whole shop feels like the Great North. You'll
want to cuddle in the oversized sweaters and
maybe show off your ability to pronounce the
designers' names right! The little courtyard behind
the shop is the scene of ephemeral showrooms
which blossom like snowdrops. The atmosphere
is cordial and the welcome warm: feel free to have
a fashion talk!
*Sweater (€230)*

# [thecollection]
DESIGN & OBJECTS

**33 Rue de Poitou, 3rd • M° Filles-du-Calvaire
www.thecollection.fr
Tuesday-Saturday 12-7 pm**

Stickers, lamps, wallpaper, and amazing design ideas, coming mainly from young British designers.
*Wallpaper kit (€42)*

# Tools Galerie
DESIGN

**119 Rue Vieille-du-Temple, 3rd • M° Filles-du-Calvaire
www.toolsgalerie.com
Tuesday-Friday 11 am-1 pm and 2:30-7 pm;
Saturday 11 am-7 pm**

An exciting selection of contemporary design from all around the world.

# Trésor by
FASHION (WOMEN)

**6 Rue du Trésor, 4th • M° Hôtel-de-Ville
Tuesday-Sunday 11 am-7:30 pm**

This fabulous store is located in the cul-de-sac of the Rue du Trésor. Colorful prints and accessories, creative, ultra-feminine designs, and great fashion advice.
*Dress (around €200)*

My addresses around Marais and Châtelet
_____
_____
_____
_____
_____
_____
_____

# 3.

# The Quartier Latin, Saint-Germain-des-Prés and Montparnasse

You probably already know the Latin Quarter and Saint-Germain-des-Prés: who doesn't? It's one of the postcards of Paris, buzzing with students and sidewalk cafés. Also the heart of the intellectual establishment, it swarms with prestigious publishers, philosophers, journalists, artists and actors: the chattering classes, as they say in London. Struggling artists were priced out of the Montparnasse real-estate market decades ago, but a few galleries surived on Rue Campagne-Première, and theatres still entertain crowds on the Rue de la Gaîté. Josephine Baker and the années folles may merely be a distant echo, but there are little-known nooks to explore in nearby Luxembourg Gardens, and a stroll around Montparnasse Cemetery is not at all morbid.

# Parisians' Secret Eateries

## The Quartier Latin and Saint-Germain-des-Prés

### Pères et Filles

FRENCH ◆◆

**81 Rue de Seine, 6th • M° Mabillon • 01 43 25 00 28**
**Daily 12-2:30 pm and 7-11 pm**

The long Rue de Seine is still one of the most pleasant strolls in the area. This family bistro features classical French cuisine, with starters like cucumber, chèvre, and basil mille-feuille, followed by beef tartare, tuna, or magret de canard. The setting is also traditional, with white tiles and globes, books and postcards. You'll be welcomed by a cheerful staff of polite, friendly waiters, qualities that bear mentioning in Paris!

### Le Timbre

FRENCH ◆◆

**3 Rue Sainte-Beuve, 6th • M° Vavin • 01 45 49 10 40**
**Tuesday-Saturday 12-1.30 pm and 7:30-10:15 pm**

This quintessential French bistro has few tables to offer, and the menu is also limited by the discriminating chef, who will only serve the freshest ingredients on the market. Forewarned is forearmed: to enjoy the amazing flavors of this quaint little eatery, either make a reservation or come early.

### Quai Quai

FRENCH ◆◆

**74 Quai des Orfèvres, 1st • M° Pont-Neuf or Saint-Michel • 01 46 33 69 75**
**Tuesday-Saturday at lunch and dinner**

There are two entrances to this trendy yet simple typical Parisian address: one is on the waterfront, and the other is on the Place Dauphine. But there is only one way to enjoy it: have the fabulous lentil salad as a starter and a delicate spinach risotto as a main course! Or better yet, do as you please!

## Ze Kitchen Gallery
FRENCH ◆◆

**4 Rue des Grands-Augustins, 6th • M° Saint-Michel • 01 44 32 00 32**
**Monday-Friday 12-2:30 pm and 7-11 pm; Saturday 7-11 pm**

Clearly one of THE places to eat in Paris at the moment. Fabulous food meets fine art in a studio that's also a restaurant and a gallery. The chef offers an inventive Asian-inspired cuisine. Everybody raves about it, so why not you?

## Les Papilles
FRENCH ◆◆

**30 Rue Gay-Lussac, 5th • RER Luxembourg**
**01 43 25 20 79**
**Monday-Saturday 12-2 pm and 7:30-10 pm**

A bistro buzzing with conviviality: foie gras or snails are a southwestern French prelude to huge salads, but try out the "retour du marché," a selection of the best products of the season picked up at the market. Very chic with a glass of fine wine...

## Chez les Filles
NORTH AFRICAN ◆

**64 Rue du Cherche-Midi, 6th • M° Sèvres-Babylone • 01 45 48 61 54**
**Monday-Friday 11:30 am-4:30 pm; Saturday 11:30 am-6:30 pm**

This small and sunny restaurant features family-style cooking from Morocco, Tunisia, and Algeria: couscous and tajines, but also veggie plates, all with the "je ne sais quoi" of Oriental spice and splendor. The wonderful smells are an invitation to hop the Mediterranean and visit its southern shore.

**+** Avoid the kebabs in la Rue de la Huchette unless you're leaving a late showing of **The Rocky Horror Picture Show** at the Studio Galande. 42 Rue Galande, 5th • 01 43 54 72 71. Every Friday and Saturday at 10 pm. Don't forget your rice and a small bottle of water!

## Le Délicabar

FRENCH ◆◆

**Le Bon Marché • 26 Rue de Sèvres, 6th • M° Sèvres-Babylone**
**Monday-Friday 9:30 am-7 pm; Saturday 9:30 am-8 pm**

An ideal lunch spot for the famished shopper, Delicabar bills itself as a snack chic, which basically means creative food in a high-design space. Just upstairs from the Grande Epicerie, a luxury world supermarket on the ground floor of Le Bon Marché department store, it's a spacious restaurant with a terrace. Club sandwiches or salads will fill you up, but save room for dessert: heaven can wait, and macaroons are divine!

## Positano

ITALIAN ◆◆

**15 Rue des Canettes, 6th • M° Mabillon • 01 43 26 01 62**
**Daily for lunch and dinner, except Monday and Saturday**

The top pasta-and-pizza joint in the Saint-Germain area! Space is at a premium, though, so remember to make reservations. Splurge on a pizza, and then walk off the carbs by wandering around the neighborhood. If you're lucky, you'll get lost and then found again.

## L'Entrecôte

FRENCH ◆◆

**20 Rue Saint-Benoît, 6th**
**M° Saint-Germain-des-Prés • 01 45 49 16 00**
**Daily 12-14:30 pm and 7:30-11:30 pm**

Quite the institution! For 20 years, this bistro has been serving a single menu consisting of tender beef, the best fries in the city, and a delicious sauce. Every day, Parisians stand in line to relish these simple delights.

## Le Jardin des Pâtes

ORGANIC PASTA ◆

**4 Rue Lacépède, 5th • M° Place-Monge • 01 43 31 50 71**
**Daily 12-14 pm and 19-23 pm**

A guilt-free pasta treat! The noodles are made fresh daily from organic wheat flour combined with various other grains and nuts, such as rice, barley, rye, or chestnut. The dishes are simply delicious, full of cheeses, ham, veggies... With its stone walls and simple wooden furniture, the place itself has a familiar feeling, kinda like coming back home.

## Le Comptoir Relais Saint-Germain

FRENCH ◆◆

**9 Carrefour de l'Odéon, 6th • M° Odéon**
**01 44 27 07 97 (no reservation, long wait)**
**Brasserie: Monday-Friday 12-6 pm; Saturday-Sunday 12-11 pm**
**Restaurant: Monday-Friday 8:30-11 pm**

The "It" chef in Paris right now, Yves Camdeborde, is dazzling diners with some of the finest food in town, in this pocket-sized restaurant down the street from the Place de l'Odéon. True, it's a challenge to score a table, but if you do succeed, you may as well go all-out and order the exquisite Menu Gastronomique (€42), heavenly from soup to nuts!

## Le Gorille Blanc

FRENCH ◆◆

**11 bis Rue Chomel, 7th • M° Sèvres-Babylone • 01 45 49 04 54**
**Daily 12-2.30 pm and 7-10.30 pm**

Le Gorille Blanc is one of the precious addresses in the Bon Marché area. The chef is a veteran of the top-of-the-line Hôtel Crillon. What he offers here is simple family fare, but with a twist of sophistication and cosmopolitanism: purple asparagus with hazelnut vinaigrette, ginger-roasted salmon with Jerusalem-artichoke bread, and strawberry soup. Quiet but fashionable, outstanding qualities in this busy shopping district.

# Around Montparnasse

## Le Café d'Enfer

FRENCH ◆◆

**22 Rue Daguerre, 14th • M° Denfert-Rochereau**
**www.cafedenfer.com • 01 43 22 23 75**
**Daily 12-2 pm and 7-11 pm; Sunday brunch 11 am-2 pm**

A good place to kick back and watch the passing crowds on the Rue Daguerre pedestrian mall, the Café d'Enfer is a family bistro. In a black-and-white ambience highlighted with flashy pictures of flamenco dancers, you can begin a hearty meal with cream of asparagus soup, followed by grilled fresh tuna with ginger and lime caramel, with a side of mashed potatoes. Some people say it's a celebrity hangout, but we aren't ones to kiss and tell.

## L'Apollo

FRENCH ◆◆

**3 Place Denfert-Rochereau, 14th • M° Denfert-Rochereau**
**www.restaurant-apollo.com • 01 45 38 76 77**
**Daily 12-3 pm and 7 pm-12 am**

If you're hankering for wide-open spaces with your meal, or have a large party to seat, run to Apollo, located in a former train-station lobby. Its great volumes are filled with comfy Pop design seats, and you can take the sun on the quiet terrace. Fish is the star of the clean French "new-bistro" fare; the tomato mille-feuille is a sophisticated starter; desserts are simple; and everything is superbly prepared.

## L'Entêtée

FRENCH ◆

**4 Rue Danville, 14th • M° Denfert Rochereau • 01 40 47 56 81**
**Tuesday-Friday 12:30-2:30 pm and 7-11 pm; Saturday 7-11 pm only**

Stubborn: that's the name of this restaurant, and we can tell you that in the kitchen, stubbornness is a virtue. The menu is basic, but deliciously prepared and well served. Try the Parmentier de Canard, for example... the mashed potatoes taste like your own grandmother made them.

## Britanny in Paris

CRÊPERIES ◆

Crêpe-making is an art which provides the cook with many forms of expression. You must sample the sit-down crêperies surrounding the Gare Montparnasse, where the trains from rural Brittany, the home of this thin pancake, brought fresh-faced young Bretons to Paris seeking work. A crêpe meal is symphony with two themes: savory and sweet. The overture enchants you: prepared in the Brittany tradition with buckwheat flour, and filled with cheese, ham, sausage, eggs, or vegetables. The sweet part is to die for: from simple butter and sugar crêpes to those oozing chocolate sauce, ice cream and crème Chantilly. Be sure to order the tangy hard cider, which is also a Brittany tradition.

Here are a couple of addresses (M° Montparnase-Bienvenüe). Prices range from €5 to €8 per crêpe.

- **Crêperie de Pont-Aven: 54 Rue du Montparnasse, 14th**
- **Crêperie de Saint-Malo: 53 Rue du Montparnasse, 14th**
- **Le Petit Josselin: 59 Rue du Montparnasse, 14th**
- **Crêperie de Josselin: 67 Rue du Montparnasse, 14th**

# The Night Time is the Right Time

**A** good-natured mixture of chic nightspots and after-match rugby parties keeps the neighborhood hopping. It's where the "wannabee cool" crowds gather.

## The Quartier Latin and Saint-Germain-des-Prés

### La Palette

DRINKS

**43 Rue de Seine, 6th • M° Odéon**
**01 43 26 68 15 • Daily 9-2 am**

La Palette is a Left Bank must, with a large terrace asserting its right to occupy a hunk of the exclusive Rue de Seine. Locals mix it up with flocks of tourists. Order a strong "espresso serré," and you'll have plenty of energy to explore the art galleries and antique shops in the rest of the neighborhood.

Enjoy the sun while young artists search for inspiration in the courtyard of the **École des Beaux-Arts**. Neoclassical statues, trees, a fountain: the Renaissance lives, along with La Bohème and liberty.

**École des Beaux-Arts:**
**14 Rue Bonaparte, 6th**
**M° Saint-Germain-des-Prés**

### Le Lup

DRINKS

**2 Rue du Sabot, 6th • M° Saint-Germain-des-Prés**
**www.lelup.com • 01 45 48 86 47**
**Daily 9 pm-5 am**

The Lup is one of the latest Parisian flings. A former brothel (or lupanar), it is starting a new life as an all-night restaurant and bar, having freshened up its rococo red interior. It's an upmarket venue, so don't expect to be welcomed here wearing flip-flops. The combination of cocktails, dining, and live jazz and funk magnifies Paris's wee hours.

# Le Bar du Marché

DRINKS

**75 Rue de Seine, 6th • M° Mabillon • 01 43 26 55 15**
**Daily 7:30-2 am**

This bar has one of the most coveted terraces in the city, and you'll be lucky to get a table! But do try, because it is a quintessential Parisian experience: everyone knows the place. It opens onto a pedestrian mall near the Marché Saint-Germain, surrounded by amenities like florists, bakeries, and restaurants. The casual bourgeois crowd that hangs out there is always up for a pastis before dinner!

## Dance outdoors on the waterfront

From May to September, every evening (though weekends are prime time) when the weather is fine, the waterfront garden on **Square Tino-Rossi**, just below Quai Saint-Bernard and the Institut du Monde Arabe in the 5th arrondissement, comes alive as an open-air dance pavilion, starting at either 7 or 9 pm. Learn to do the tango, waltz, or java under the starry skies of Paris. Absolutely not to be missed. And free, though the musicians do appreciate tips.

# La Crèmerie

WINE BAR

**9 Rue des Quatre-Vents, 6th • M° Odéon • 01 43 54 99 30**
**Tuesday-Thursday 4:30-10 pm and Friday-Saturday 12.30-3 pm**

This former dairy store is 130 years old. It became a wine cellar in the 1950s, and has been a genuine, old-fashioned wine bar ever since, a monument to oenology. Now it specializes in natural wines, artisan cheeses, and rural French sausages, pâtés, and hams. A perfect place for friends to meet for drinks before dinner.

My addresses around Quartier Latin and Saint-Germain-des-Prés

## Around Montparnasse

### Le Café Tournesol
DRINKS

**9 Rue de la Gaîté, 6th • M° Edgar-Quinet or Gaîté • 01 43 27 65 72**
**Monday-Saturday 8:30-1:30 am and Sunday 9:30-1:30 am; food served until 11 pm**

It is certainly a treat to find such a welcoming establishment in this neighborhood, right in the heart of the Rue de la Gaîté theater district. Bop to the electro-jazz background music around a beer with friends. The focus of the menu is simple southwestern cuisine (and we don't mean tacos). The chocolate cake is to die for!

### Le Petit Journal Montparnasse
DRINKS & LIVE MUSIC

**13 Rue du Commandant-René-Mouchotte, 14th**
**M° Gaîté or Montparnasse-Bienvenüe • 01 43 21 56 70**
**Monday-Saturday 7-2 am**

Art-deco brasserie by day, club by night, this is an address for lovers of eclectic music! On weeknights, have a drink to the sound of French golden oldies. And on weekends, enjoy the jazz, swing, and big band pizzazz. Concerts start at 10 pm.

## ✚ Let's be snobs!

A few tips, just in case a Parisian invites you to his home for dinner:
• Always be at least a half-hour late.
• Don't arrive empty-handed: present your host or hostess with flowers, a bottle of wine, or a small gift (a Parigramme guide, for instance!)
• Dress up: it's the occasion to strut your new Parisian finery, and you never know where the night may lead.
• Remember, money is a taboo subject. It's like sex: everyone thinks about it, but they're usually too hypocritical to talk about it.

# Culture mix

The Latin Quarter and Montparnasse have outgrown their devil-may-care youth and acquired major museums with eye-catching architecture, enticing programs, and the deep pockets necessary for such attractions. But there's still a melody of insouciance and spontaneity in the narrow streets, where artists perform and pass the hat. As for film entertainment, the Latin Quarter art houses attract cinephiles from all over the city, the country, and possibly the world.

## Legendary Saint-Germain-des-Prés

The first building to rise in this area on the Left Bank of the Seine was a monastery, built to shelter a trophy the Merovingian King Childebert I brought back from Pamplona in 542, the tunic of Saint Vincent, patron saint of vintners. Gradually, the settlement grew. In the 18th century, the neighborhood became a gathering place for Enlightenment philosophers; the walls of the Café Procope, which is still doing business, reverberated with new ideas. Intellectual and artistic effervescence continued to fizz throughout the 19th century, when Delacroix and Manet dwelt here, and reached another peak in the 20th. In the 1920s, the fashionable literary circles and cafés became mythical. Jean-Paul Sartre and Simone de Beauvoir held court at Brasserie Lipp and the Cafés Flore and Deux Magots, where their followers drank in their words, along with their tea. After World War Two, the jazz scene flourished in the vaulted cellars of the area, filled with the melodic inventions and improvisations of such greats as

Duke Ellington, Miles Davis, and Sidney Bechet. Existentialism ruled, as singer Juliette Gréco became the muse of Paris's equivalent of Greenwich Village. French Zazous, bebop artists, and immortal songwriters like Léo Ferré, Serge Gainsbourg, and Jacques Brel kept the endless nights sparkling with wit and laughter. Nowadays, some excellent bookstores (open late into the night) continue the philosophical tradition, but more and more shops are selling out to designer boutiques... But then again, it did all start with a tunic, after all!

# The Quartier Latin and Saint-Germain-des-Prés

## Institut du Monde Arabe
ARAB CULTURE

**1 Rue des Fossés-Saint-Bernard, place Mohammed-V, 5th**
**M° Jussieu, Cardinal-Lemoine or Sully-Morland**
**www.imarabe.org • 01 40 51 38 38 • Admission: €8**
**Tuesday-Sunday 10 am-6 pm**

A monolithic Parisian tribute to Arabic culture and arts and the deep historical bonds linking France and the Mediterranean world. If you are passionate
or even simply curious about Arabic and Islamic cultures, you will surely enjoy
the rich collection of art, the musical and
dance performances, or the temporary
exhibits. These events all take place inside an
incredible contemporary building on the Left
Bank of the Seine, designed by architect Jean
Nouvel. Head to the top floor for a beautiful
view of Paris.

You can also visit the **Paris Mosque**,
built in 1922. Don't miss the traditional
Moroccan mint tea and pastries
at the Moorish-style café inside the
compound:
**Mosquée de Paris:**
**2 bis Place du Puits-de-l'Ermite, 5th**
**www.mosquee-de-paris.org**
**01 45 35 97 33**

## Cinéma du Panthéon
MOVIE THEATER

**13 Rue Victor-Cousin, 5th • RER Luxembourg • 01 40 46 01 21**
**cinema.pantheon.free.fr**

Le Panthéon recently made the news: its quaint restaurant was redecorated
by French film star and Chanel muse Catherine Deneuve. But as you dine, be
mindful of the fact that it's also one of Paris's oldest independent art houses,
totally dedicated to European movies. The names of the greatest filmmakers
of all times are engraved in the seats, so pick your favorite one!

# ✚ Time travel in Paris's narrow medieval streets

Three little strolls that will take you back to the Paris of poet François Villon, he who wondered about the snows of yesteryear...

**Tour 1**: From Métro station Cité, cross the piazza in front of Notre-Dame Cathedral and, on the northern side of the huge structure, explore Rue du Cloître-Notre-Dame, wandering left onto Rue des Chanoinesses, right on Rue de la Colombe, and then right again on Rue des Ursins.

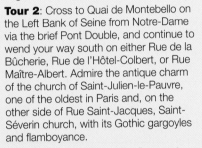

**Tour 2**: Cross to Quai de Montebello on the Left Bank of Seine from Notre-Dame via the brief Pont Double, and continue to wend your way south on either Rue de la Bûcherie, Rue de l'Hôtel-Colbert, or Rue Maître-Albert. Admire the antique charm of the church of Saint-Julien-le-Pauvre, one of the oldest in Paris and, on the other side of Rue Saint-Jacques, Saint-Séverin church, with its Gothic gargoyles and flamboyance.

**Tour 3**: Right Bank medievalism centers on the Rue des Barres, which rises from Pont Louis-Philippe and skirts the back of Saint-Gervais church.

## Musée National du Moyen Âge, Thermes et Hôtel de Cluny
MEDIEVAL ART

**6 Place Paul-Painlevé, 5th • M° Saint-Michel**
**www.musee-moyenage.fr • 01 53 73 78 00**
**Wednesday-Monday 9:15 am-6 pm • Admission: €7.50 (audio guide included);**
**€5.50 for those 18-25.**
**Free for visitors under 18 and for all, on the 1st Sunday of every month.**

There are many reasons to visit the national museum of the Middle Ages, which includes Gallo-Roman baths, the medieval dwelling of the Abbotts of Cluny, and an impressive collection of medieval stained glass and sculpture. The centerpiece of the tour remains the six famed Lady and the Unicorn tapestries, guaranteed to cast a spell on you. Maximize the magic by avoiding the week-end crowds.

# Around Montparnasse

## Musée Bourdelle
SCULPTURE

**18 Rue Antoine-Bourdelle, 15th • M° Falguière**
**01 49 54 73 73**
**Tuesday-Sunday 10 am-6 pm. Admission: Free**

Antoine Bourdelle (1861-1929) is a French sculptor who attracted the admiration of the famed Auguste Rodin. Bourdelle's former studio, on a quiet street, is off the beaten tourist track and free of crowds. It is also a journey through sculpture and mythology. The museum often features special shows by contemporary artists as well.

## Musée Zadkine
SCULPTURE

**100 bis Rue d'Assas, 6th**
**M° Notre-Dame-des-Champs**
**01 55 42 77 20**
**Tuesday-Sunday Daily 10 am-6 pm.**
**Admission: Free**

Ossip Zadkine (1890-1967), a wanderer from Russia, settled in Paris after attending art school in London. The collection shows his evolution from an interest in Cubism to the late years in the 1960s. His studio, with its peaceful garden, is a haven.

## Musée du Montparnasse
THE BOHÈME

**21 Avenue du Maine, 15th • M° Montparnasse-Bienvenüe**
**www.museedumontparnasse.net • 01 42 22 91 96**
**Tuesday-Sunday 12:30-7 pm • Admission: €5**

The small dead-end street where the museum is located is still haunted by the spirits of the penniless young artists who were driven to become the most important painters, sculptors, and writers of the early 20th century (Picasso, Matisse, Modigliani, Apollinaire, Aragon, Cocteau). Painter Marie Vassilieff ran a restaurant for hungry artists here, during the gloomy war years, 1915 to 1918, and the Bohemian atmosphere has been religiously kept alive. The museum welcomes temporary exhibitions in this vein: visits, lectures, and also parties.

## Fondation Cartier pour l'Art Contemporain
CONTEMPORARY ART EXHIBITIONS

**261 Boulevard Raspail, 14th • M° Raspail or Denfert-Rochereau**
**www.fondation.cartier.com • 01 42 18 56 50 ("Nomades" nights 01 42 18 56 72)**
**Admission: €6.50**
**Tuesday-Sunday 11 am-8 pm; Tuesdays until 10 pm. Closed January 1st,**
**May 1st, and December 25th**

The Fondation Cartier is a private foundation initiated by Cartier, the world-renowned French jeweler. For over twenty years, Cartier has been a patron of contemporary artists from all over the world, organizing exhibitions and financing art projects. In 1994, the Foundation opened a modern exhibition space designed by Jean Nouvel, introducing contemporary architecture on the Left Bank. Here, visitors can enjoy a diversity of art forms from photography to painting, installations, and also contemporary pop music: the Rock'n'roll exhibit was a Parisian hangout in 2007, and everybody was talking about the Foundation's presentation of Patti Smith in 2008! Every Thursday night, it hosts a Soirée Nomade, featuring a live performer or a happening. Check the website for the schedule. Reservations are mandatory!

## ✚ A city for cinema lovers

Parisians go to the movies at least once a week, so why not join them? A few rules though: for showtimes, buy the Pariscope or L'Officiel from any newsstand or go online www.allocine.fr. Always get there at least a half hour before the screening (15 minutes before the film). Make sure you choose the right language: it's either VF (dubbed in French) or VO (the original language with French subtitles). And then, just enjoy!

## Fondation Henri Cartier-Bresson
PHOTO EXHIBITIONS

**2 Impasse Lebouis,14th • M° Gaîté or Edgar-Quinet**
**www.henricartierbresson • 01 56 80 27 00**

The sharp eye of the great Henri Cartier-Bresson made photographic poetry out of every landmark event of his lifetime, from the rising fascist peril in the 1930s, when he sympathized with the Spanish Republicans, the subjugation of Paris under the Occupation and the euphoria of the liberation. He also traced the rise and fall of the French colonial myth, used his lens to examine the world's antagonistic ideologies, and, in short, ushered in the century of the image. Lastly, his portraits immortalized the celebrities of his time: Camus, Sartre, Faulkner, Mauriac, and so many others. The Foundation alternates presentations of Cartier-Bresson's work with that of other artists.

# Shopping French Bourgeois

Taking off from Métro Sèvres-Babylone, enjoy a couple of hours of shopping in the 6th arrondissement, the spot for bourgeois spending in the heart of intellectual Left-Bank Paris. You'll find everything from bras to bookshops…

**Icons:** Charlotte Gainsbourg and Louis Garrel, actors

### Paul & Joe
FASHION (WOMEN/CHILDREN)

**66 Rue des Saints-Pères, 6th • M° Sèvres-Babylone
Monday-Saturday 10 am-7 pm**

Decoration meets fashion in this boudoir: it's like entering the dressing room of a very fashionable girlfriend, a bit baroque but as cozy as a teatime rendezvous. Don't let the prices impress you: the clothes are very eclectic and the total look is possible. Paul & Joe represents the "it" of style for many Parisians: comfortable, a bit chic with a bohemian touch... Sweet!
*High silver boots (€585) / Silk top (€210)*

### BA&SH
FASHION (WOMEN)

**80 Rue des Saints-Pères, 7th • M° Sèvres-Babylone
Monday-Saturday 10:30am-7:30 pm**

A cute brand, somewhat styley, BA&SH proposes fashion for women: blue jeans, blouses, and sweaters, slightly bohemian, very feminine. Their best-seller: a leather jacket.
*Top (around €75) / Leather jacket (€350)*

### Tara Jarmon
FASHION (WOMEN)

**75 Rue des Saints-Pères, 7th • M° Sèvres-Babylone
Monday-Saturday 11 am-7 pm**

The classic brand Tara Jarmon is your average French womenswear: sophisticated dresses, Jackie O jackets, classy pants. Great if you're looking for a dress for a special occasion!
*Dress (from €150)*

# Iro
FASHION (WOMEN)

**68 Rue des Saints-Pères, 7th • M° Sèvres-Babylone**

Very hip, IRO has a special contemporary touch: sober colors, soft silks, fine woolens, and a little something trendy. Simple tees with bold graphics are difficult to resist!
*Dress (€120)*

# Claudie Pierlot
FASHION (WOMEN)

**23 Rue du Vieux-Colombier, 6th • M° Sèvres-Babylone**
**Monday-Friday 10:30 am-7 pm; Saturday 10:30 am-7:30**

Are you the kind of girl who falls for clothes with beautiful details? Then you'll be spellbound by Claudie Pierlot: simple fashion with a little "je ne sais quoi" guaranteed to capture your heart. Smart buttons, round collars, inventive draping, large pockets, just-right lengths... A sensitive touch also mirrored by a trendy selection of accessories.
*Woolen skirt (€155) / Low boots (€190)*

## ✚ Let's be snobs!

Treat yourself to an Ispahan (a divine combination of fresh raspberries and lychees inside a beautiful pink rosewater-flavored macaroon) at **Pierre Hermé's designer-pastry boutique**. Hermé is so daring, innovative, and full of genius that he has been dubbed "the Picasso of pastry" in the US press. Have it wrapped to go, and savor it on the Place Saint-Sulpice.

**Pierre Hermé: 72 Rue Bonaparte, 6th**
**M° Saint-Sulpice or Saint-Placide**

# Agnès B.
FASHION (WOMEN/MEN)

**6 & 12 Rue du Vieux-Colombier, 6th • M° Saint-Placide**
**Monday-Saturday 10 am-7:30 pm**

Agnès B. is a graphic and minimalist brand famous for its basics. B-lovers see these clothes as essentials because of the precision of their cut and the way they drape. They're the perfect illustration of the expression "un rien l'habille" ("she looks dressed up with anything"). The modern less-is-more esthetic is also expressed by the boutique décor. The designer herself, a prominent photography collector, has endowed her gallery-like spaces with a personal touch.
*Cotton cardigan (€70) / Lambswool dress (€135)*

## Zadig & Voltaire
FASHION (WOMEN/MEN/CHILDREN)

**1-3 Rue du Vieux-Colombier, 6th • M° Saint-Placide**
**Tuesday-Saturday 10:30 am-7:30 pm; Monday 1-7:30 pm**

Caution… You are entering the ultimate bourgeois address. Wealthy Parisians frequently drop in and leave with the latest sweater… Simple in form (all necklines), color (pastels meet grayish tones), and fabric (all wools and cashmere!), they're eminently collectable… The brand surfs on the decorative graphics trend and its Goth/glamrock roots: designs and messages showing you're a member of the Zadig community are emblazoned on the backs of the sweaters. Now the whole family can join the tribe!
*Printed t-shirt (€80) / Round-neck cashmere sweater (€255)*

## Joseph
FASHION (WOMEN)

**68 Rue Bonaparte, 6th • M° Saint-Placide**
**Monday-Saturday 10:30 am-7 pm**

Girls say it's the best place in town to purchase a perfectly-fitted pair of trousers. Of course, they won't catch your eye when you go in, but try some on, and you'll be an instant convert. Joseph is a subtle brand that insistently whispers quality: the dresses suit any girl whose natural beauty serves as the foundation for the simple shapes. This designer puts the spotlight on you, not what you're wearing.
*Dress (€293) / Pants (€248)*

## Cacharel
FASHION (WOMEN/MEN/CHILDREN)

**64 Rue Bonaparte, 6th • M° Saint-Placide**
**Monday-Friday 10:30 am-7 pm; Saturday 10:30 am-7:30 pm**

Founded in the 1960s, Cacharel has embarked on a new era. The store is an all-white space reminiscent of the Beatles' 1968 album, placing the focus on product, not packaging. Cacharel's trademark romantic charm is still evident in its floral-print dresses, soft sweaters, and classically tasteful coats.
*Dress (€250)*

## Dinh Van
JEWELRY

**56 Rue Bonaparte, 6th • M° Saint-Placide**
**Tuesday-Saturday 10:45 am-7 pm; Monday 1-7 pm**

Dinh Van achieved Paris fame with his lifesaver-shaped Kamasoutra pendant on a colored nylon cord: every self-respecting rich girl wore one as a bracelet. These days, the designer offers a range of modern, sensual pieces with the same talismanic power. The rings are a far cry from Tiffany's, but they also have something more magical about them. "I want my jewelry to take to the streets," Dinh Van told reporters. Mission accomplished!
*Silver pendant (€210) / White gold & diamond ring (€2100)*

## Le Bon Marché
DEPARTMENT STORE

**24 Rue de Sèvres, 7th**
**M° Sèvres-Babylone**
**Monday, Tuesday and Wednesday 10 am-7:30 pm;**
**Thursday 10 am-9 pm; Friday 10 am-8 pm;**
**Saturday 9:30 am-8 pm**

This historical department store is practically a monument to Left Bank elegance. Smoother and quieter than the other Parisian department stores, Le Bon Marché is an engraved invitation to fashion, decoration, beauty, and stationery. The ground floor of the second store is an awesome international food emporium called La Grande Epicerie; upstairs, you'll find ladies' fashion. Le Bon Marché is no place to go bargain-hunting. It's not "bon marché" (affordable), but it is an experience.

## Monoprix
FASHION (WOMEN/MEN/CHILDREN)

**50 Rue de Rennes, 6th • M° Saint-Germain-des-Prés**
**www.monoprix.fr • Monday-Saturday 9 am-10 pm**

Monoprix is the go-to store for basics: food, cosmetics, and... fashion! The racks are filled with simple clothes in a wide range of sizes, and always offer pleasant surprises: up-to-date casuals at decent prices. Designers are occasionally invited in to do star turns. The hosiery and lingerie departments are also well worth browsing. This particular Monoprix has an especially good ladies' wear department.
*Sweater (€39.90)*

# 4.
# Invalides

Welcome to the upmarket side of Paris, populated by high-ranking government officials, ambassadors, the affluent classes, and the minority of Parisians fortunate enough to share a view of the Invalides or Eiffel Tower. Like most wealthy enclaves, it is largely quiet, green, and residential. To be honest, it's a bit dull. Shhhh!

# Parisians' Secret Eateries

## L'Ami Jean
SOUTHWEST FRENCH ◆◆

**27 Rue Malar, 7th • M° La Tour-Maubourg • 01 47 05 86 89**
**Tuesday-Saturday 12-2 pm and 7 pm-12 am**

Let's start with a little context: southwestern France is known for its rugby teams, excellent cuisine, and regional chauvinism. Sample the essence of this distinctive culture with a dinner at L'Ami Jean. What's on the menu? Bayonne cured ham, similar to prosciutto; potted duck, small potatoes sautéed in duck fat, farm pigeon... an array of fresh ingredients prepared with love and Basque talent!

## Le Cristal de Sel
FRENCH ◆◆

**13 Rue Mademoiselle, 15th • M° Commerce • 01 42 50 35 29**
**Tuesday-Saturday 12:30-2:30 pm and 7-10:30 pm**

Hello gastronomy! You've come to the right place to savour gourmet French cuisine. A former chef from the upscale Hôtel Bristol opened this sober and nonetheless charming restaurant to offer a slate full of delightful dishes, such as the ravioles with langoustines and cabbage, the sea bass garnished with eggplant caviar, or the girolle mushroom risotto. Feel free to indulge in this fine food, but don't let the check ruin your digestion!

## El Fares
LEBANESE ◆

**166 Boulevard de Grenelle, 15th • M° Cambronne • 01 47 83 54 38**
**Daily 11 am-16 pm and 7 pm-12 am**

French people love Lebanese cuisine! This spot, recommended by Lebanese friends, is family-owned and simple. The classical mezze plate, with its sample of each delicacy, is priced at €12: a great way to experience Middle-Eastern food! El Fares is neither chic nor trendy, with a strictly no-frills interior decoration scheme. But the food is delicious, served quickly and perfectly by gentlemen with adorable smiles... .

## Le Grand Venise
ITALIAN ◆ ◆ ◆

**171 Rue de la Convention, 15th • M° Convention • 01 45 32 49 71**
**Tuesday-Saturday 12 pm-2 pm and 7:30 pm-10:30 pm**

Possibly the best Italian restaurant in the city, even if few Parisians know about it. Old-fashioned pride in professionalism is the driving force in this family-owned restaurant, where the Mamma still prepares her own pasta every day.

The food is sublime (the assortments of antipasti are spectacular, and leave room for the homemade caramel ice cream) and the evening unforgettable. For a special occasion, since it is quite pricey. The fresh flower arrangements are magnificent.

# ✚ Déjeuner sur l'herbe

Here are a few ideal **picnic spots**. Grab a fresh baguette at the *boulangerie* and then hit the *charcuterie* for salads, a rôtisserie chicken, perhaps, or sliced meat or cheese. If you buy wine there, they'll uncork it for you; all you have to do is say *s'il vous plaît*. Then head for the hills!

## Pont des Arts
**M° Louvre-Rivoli**

This graceful iron footbridge spanning the Seine between the Cour Carrée of the Louvre and the Institut de France is one of the most romantic strolls in town. It is thoughtfully equipped with benches, where picnickers celebrate the beauty of Paris by toasting the city al fresco. From the Left Bank, shop the Rue de Buci market. Unfortunately, on the Right, you'll have to hike a long way to find a fresh tomato.
Access: Quai du Louvre/François-Mitterrand or Quai Malaquais/Quai de Conti

## Invalides
**7th • M° Invalides**

A flat piece of grassy land between the Seine and the Invalides, the Esplanade attracts soccer and rugby amateurs as well as picnickers. But there's plenty of room for everyone. Sustenance is available a bit farther to the west, on the Rue Saint-Dominique.

# Le Cinq-Mars
FRENCH ◆◆

**51 Rue de Verneuil, 7th • M° Rue-du-Bac • 01 45 44 69 13**
**Monday-Saturday 12-2:30 pm and 7:45 pm-12 am**

Typical bistro cuisine is tweaked for the 21st century at this jolly eatery practically around the corner from Orsay... Even the hard-boiled egg and mayonnaise "œuf mayo" will taste far better then at home. And, of course, the chef whips up a divine mousse au chocolat. Enjoy!

# Le Dix-Vins
FRENCH ◆

**57 Rue Falguière, 15th • M° Pasteur • 01 43 20 91 77**
**Monday-Friday 12-2:30 pm and 7:30-10:30 pm**

Menu specials change daily at this pleasant bistro. You can choose from four starters, four main courses of fish or meat, and then opt for either cheese or dessert. The regional wines in the cellar are divine, hence the punny restaurant name.

# Champ de Mars
**7th • M° École-Militaire**
Have a picnic with the Eiffel Tower as a special guest! The Champ de Mars is a vast, landscaped lawn between the Eiffel Tower and the École Militaire. At the École-Militaire Métro exit, you should be able to track down a few grocers.

# Canal Saint-Martin
**10th • M° Jacques-Bonsergent**
The Canal Saint-Martin has become a popular hangout, especially on weekends, when the streets on either side are closed to automobile traffic. The occasional activity of the locks when a barge goes by provides ample excitement for the people who gather here. Best places to picnic are the Quai de Valmy around the Rue de Marseille, and Quai de Jemmapes between the Rue de l'Hôpital-Saint-Louis and Rue Bichat. Some bars sell drinks to go (Le Poisson Rouge: 112 Quai de Jemmapes)

# Parc des Buttes-Chaumont
**19th • M° Botzaris or Pyrénées**
It's a treat to visit this big 19th-century park on Paris's northerly heights, with its variety of artificial landscapes. It offers a wonderful view from the "Belvedere of Sybil," which stands on a large rock in the heart of the park. You'll find food being sold on the Rue de Belleville.
Access: Rue de Crimée, Rue Manin or Rue Botzaris.

# The Night Time is the Right Time

The 7th is hardly a major nightlife destination, with the one exception below. Otherwise, it's a residential area where the bars close early.

## Péniche Concorde Atlantique
DANCING

**23 Quai Anatole-France, 7th • 01 47 05 71 03**
**M° Assemblée-Nationale or Concorde or RER Musée-d'Orsay**

This boat is always rocking till sunrise with something going on! The trendiest parties in the city are hosted on its large deck terrace and two lower decks.

# Culture Mix

The arrival of the Quai Branly Museum a few years ago shook up the neighborhood cocktail in a major way. You must see it. The romantic pre-Branly sights, the Rodin Museum and Garden and the Chinese Pagoda, are also well worth a visit...

## Musée Rodin
SCULPTURE

**79 Rue de Varenne, 7th • M° Varenne or Invalides or Saint-François-Xavier**
**01 44 18 61 10 • Tuesday-Saturday 9:30 am-5:45 pm (4:45 pm from October to March)**
**Admission to the Museum and Garden: €6 (free on the 1st Sunday of the month)**
**Garden only: €1**

Facing considerable opposition in his own time, sculptor Auguste Rodin (1840-1917) put the human passion back into an art which had become stodgy and formulaic. He is considered the father of modern sculpture. Contemplate his best-known works (The Kiss, The Thinker, The Burghers of Calais, The Gates of Hell) to your heart's content, and then lose yourself in your own thoughts about life, art, and love in the garden, an oasis of quiet.

## La Pagode

CHINESE STYLE CINEMA

**57 Rue de Babylone, 7th • M° Saint-François-Xavier**
**01 45 55 48 48 • Tickets: €5-8**

In 1895, the owner of the Bon Marché department store had this Chinese pagoda built for his wife. They held magnificent parties there... until she left him. In the 1930s, during the golden age of moviemaking, the Pagoda became a cinema, and remains an independent art house to this day. Give yourself time to take a quick tour of the Asian garden before the film, and choose Salle 1, just for the charm of its auditorium (Salle 2 is a modern theater in the basement). It's enchanting, with golden Oriental walls and chandeliers, deep red seats, and timeless atmosphere. The magic of the place will cast a spell on you, and you might just feel... in the mood for love!

## Musée du Quai Branly

PRIMITIVE ART

**37 Quai Branly, 7th • M° Iéna or Alma-Marceau or Bir-Hakeim or RER Pont-de-l'Alma**
**www.quaibranly.fr • 01 56 61 70 00 • Admission: €8.50**
**Tuesday, Wednesday and Sunday 11 am-7 pm; Thursday, Friday and Saturday 11 am-9 pm. Closed May 1st and December 25th.**

This enormous building, designed by star architect Jean Nouvel and opened in 2006, is a dramatic departure from its classical Parisian surroundings. Visiting the museum is like walking through an organic maze filled with beau-

tiful, exotic objects. The permanent collection presents indigenous art of past civilizations of the Africa, Oceania, Asia, and the Americas. The objects are beautifully and playfully displayed in alcoves along dimly-lit, winding aisles. It is as much a cultural experience as it is a wonderful sensorial journey filled with shapes, colors, and sounds. Some have called it primitive, but in the end, it is just inspiring.

My addresses around Invalides

# 5.
# Champs-Élysées and Trocadéro

Sorry to break the news: the "most beautiful avenue in the world" is not a place Parisians enjoy, at least during the day – too many tourists, glitzy stores, and expensive restaurants. After sundown, though, they do head there to boogie in the clubs. Likewise, there are clusters of museums you may not have had time to explore your first time around Paris, and we heartily recommend them.

# Parisians'
## Secret
# Eateries

## Restaurant du Théâtre du Rond-Point
FRENCH ◆◆

**2 bis, Avenue Franklin-D.-Roosevelt, 8th • M° Franklin-D.-Roosevelt**
**01 44 95 98 44**
**Monday 12-3 pm; Tuesday-Thursday 12 pm-12 am;**
**Friday and Saturday 7:30 pm-1:30 am**

Located inside the theater, the restaurant feels like an extension of it, with a soft red and black interior and artistic mood. You'll feel comfortable in the hands of the friendly waitstaff, the food is up to the usual French high standards yet simple, and the other diners are cordial and clever. A real must to meet "intellos".

## Le PDG
AMERICAN ◆◆

**20 Rue de Ponthieu, 8th • M° Franklin-D.-Roosevelt**
**01 42 56 19 10**
**Daily 7:45 am-11 pm**

Most Parisians would never admit it, but truth be told, they LOVE hamburgers, and this joint is packed from morning till night! The PDG (Pretty Darned Good?) will satisfy your burger craving quite skillfully, and there are plenty of other dishes to choose from as well. If you're more of a "Left Banker," the PDG recently opened a branch in the Latin Quarter (5 Rue du Dragon, 6th).

## Café Carlu
FRENCH ◆

**Palais de Chaillot-Cité de l'Architecture.**
**1 Place du Trocadéro, 16th • M° Trocadéro or Iéna**
**Daily (except Tuesday) 11 am-7 pm; Thursday 11 am-9 pm**

It's still a well-kept secret, but the home of the Café Carlu happens to be one of the most beautiful spots of the city. There's nothing especially elaborate on the menu of sandwiches and salads, but the view is right on the Eiffel Tower! And, for such a thrilling location, it's quite affordable. This is strictly insider information - don't let it out.

## Tokyo Eat
ARTY WORLD ◆◆

**Palais de Tokyo: 13 Avenue du Président-Wilson, 16th
M° Iéna
www.palaisdetokyo.com • 01 47 20 00 29
Tuesday-Sunday 10 am-11 pm (summer hours);
10 am-6:30 pm (winter hours)**

The Palais de Tokyo, a raw-concrete space dedicated to contemporary art, offers a magnificent, sunny terrace to its summertime visitors. The drinks have an Asian tinge: experiment with green tea or ginger juice, to see how they combine with foie gras, carpaccios or green bean salad. For the main course, anything goes: there's risotto or pasta, beef filet with wild mushrooms or roasted salmon. The dessert menu is an unusual one: if you've had your  fill of millefeuilles by now, see how the Parisians do a milkshake. As you sip the sweetness, contemplate the Eiffel Tower. Life is tough in the 16th arrondissement!

The Tokyo Self, a cafeteria nestled on the lower floor, is a good alternative for snacking and meeting before visiting the latest show.

## Café de l'Homme
GREAT VIEW ◆◆

**Musée de l'Homme • 17 Place du Trocadéro, 16th
M° Trocadéro
www.restaurant-cafedelhomme.com • 01 44 05 30 15
Daily 12 pm-2 am**

You won't remember what you had for dinner. Your mind will still be reeling from the extraordinary view of the Eiffel Tower, standing just meters away from your table, lighting up your meal like a gigantic candle. You will have paid a little too much for the food, which though quite adequate, is nevertheless overpriced (€22 for a "homme-burger" and fries). But you will have dined in the presence of the Lady of Steel... Unique!

## Bon
FRENCH ◆◆

**25 Rue de la Pompe, 16th • M° La Muette**
**www.restaurantbon.fr • 01 40 72 70 00**
**Daily for lunch and dinner; closed for**
**lunch on Saturdays**

The dashing designer Philippe Starck created the concept interiors of this intimate bar and restaurant, a concept that could be defined as "eat fine food in a pseudo-boudoir ambience," with many a mass-produced Louis Ghost chairs, hommage to Louis XV style. The food is typical fusion fashion: organic, semi-cooked fish and seafood and tiny vegetables. If you were craving a plate of multiple chocolate delights, save room for the "Choco-bon" dessert.

## Let's be snobs!

Reserve the Baccarat restaurant's private "Cristal Room" for your birthday-party dinner. **The Baccarat flagship store**, home of the eternal crystal brand, now boasts a restaurant designed by Philippe Starck (one more!). Located in a mansion which was once the home of aristocrat and arts patron Marie-Laure de Noailles, the room dedicated to private dinner parties is all pink with ornate mirrors, a marvelous chandelier and a private balcony. Perhaps Marie-Laure's friends Salvador Dali, Balthus, and Man Ray once caroused here.
**Maison Baccarat:**
**11 Place des États-Unis, 16th • M° Kléber**
**www.baccarat.com • 01 40 22 11 10**

# The Night Time is the Right Time

**H**ighly selective VIP addresses with beautiful people wearing expensive watches and driving fancy cars coexist with tourists and young Parisians with silicone bracelets, traveling by Métro.

## BC (Black Calavados)
DANCING

**40 Avenue Pierre-Ier-de-Serbie, 8th • M° Alma-Marceau or George-V**
**www.blackcalavados.com • 01 47 20 77 77**
**Bar open every night at 12 am. Restaurant.**

Behind the doors of the 18th-century townhouse, the all-steel interior in this ultra-modern club was designed by Alexandre de Betak, famous for his fashion show designs. Despite the resolute futurism, though, they are still romantic enough to allow you to dine by a facsimile of candllelight. This club was a celebrity hangout in the 1960s and early 70s, and has been revived by Audioslave frontman Chris Cornell, who now lives in Paris. BC is in the high-rent district, so you have to dress up. It's not easy to get in, so keep cool and imagine a plan B.

**+**Also very select if you feel adventurous...

**Le ChaCha:**
**47 Rue Berger, 1st • M° Les Halles**
**www.chachaclub.fr • 01 40 13 12 12**
A gathering place for the city's beautiful people. The parties are wild, the DJ's tastes eccentric (they like to spin antiquated French pop, in an effort to bring it up to date), and the bouncers are... ruthless!

**Le Baron:**
**6 Avenue Marceau, 8th • M° Alma-Marceau**
The same owners, same vibe and, unfortunately... the same bouncers as in the above-mentioned club... We warned you!

# Le Queen
DANCING

**102 Avenue des Champs-Élysées, 8th • M° George-V**
**www.queen.fr • 01 53 89 08 90 • Every night from 11 pm**
**Cover charge: €15-20**

Long ago, this famed gay nightclub on the Champs-Élysées opened its doors to all communities and all sexes. Monday nights are dedicated to disco and Wednesday is Ladies' Night. Get ready for festive and all-night grooviness!

# Le Showcase
DANCING

**Pont Alexandre III, Port des Champs-Élysées, 8th**
**M° Champs-Élysées-Clemenceau**
**www.showcase.fr • 01 45 61 25 43**
**Daily from 10 pm • Take the stairs on the left as you face the bridge (coming from the Métro). No cover charge until 12 am; €10 afterwards.**

The Showcase is making a name for itself as a "place to be" in Paris. Located under one of the most beautiful bridges on the Seine, it has a huge dance floor where the young and wealthy shimmy and sway. It is hardly intimate and you might even have trouble getting past the velvet rope, but the spectacular setting, right on the river, is enticing.

My addresses around Champs-Élysées and Trocadéro

# Culture Mix

The best reason to go the Trocadéro or Champs-Élysées area is culture! Even east-side crowds cross town to visit the Palais de Tokyo. This contemporary-arts platform is only one of a number of cultural activities bubbling in this unlikely corner of the city. Photography, fashion, Asian art, and temporary exhibitions are among the treasures of the West. Not so boring, after all!

## Let's be snob!

Attend every auction at **Artcurial gallery**, and pretend you were just outbid on a fabulous Jean Prouvé chair...
Artcurial: 7 Rond-Point des Champs-Élysées, 8th
M° Franklin-D.-Roosevelt
Monday-Saturday 10:30 am-7 pm

## Musée du Jeu de Paume
PHOTO EXHIBITIONS

**1 Place de la Concorde, 1st • M° Concorde
01 47 03 12 50 • Admission: €6
Tuesday 12-9 pm, Wednesday-Friday 12-7 pm;
Saturday and Sunday 10 am-7 pm. Closed
January 1st, May 1st, and December 25th
The Jeu de Paume operates a second exhibition
space in the Hotel de Sully, in the Marais:
62 Rue Saint-Antoine, 4th • M° Saint-Paul
Admission: €5 • www.jeudepaume.org**

The former imperial tennis court, built in 1861, was used in later years as an exhibition space for the national collection of French Impressionists, until they were moved to the Musée d'Orsay in 1986. It opened as a national contemporary-arts museum in the 1990s, and has been devoted solely to photography and video since 2004. Its location at the western end of the Tuileries Gardens, Paris's largest, may inspire you to take a photographic walk yourself!

## Galeries Nationales du Grand Palais
ARCHITECTURAL MARVEL

**3 Avenue du Général-Eisenhower, 8th • M° Champs-Élysées-Clemenceau
www.grandpalais.fr • 01 44 13 17 17 • Admission fees vary**

Built for the 1900 Paris Exhibition, the Grand Palais is one of Paris's architectural marvels. It now houses three exhibition halls: the Palais de la Découverte, dedicated to the discovery of the sciences, (www.palais-decouverte.fr), the Galeries Nationales du Grand Palais, where the city's blockbuster art shows are usually held, and the Grande Nef, NOT to be missed, a breathtaking Eiffel-style iron-and-glass structure recently renovated and reopened. This exceptional space houses different temporary events and shows.

## Palais de Tokyo
CONTEMPORARY CREATIONS

**13 Avenue du Président-Wilson, 16th • M° Iéna**
**www.palaisdetokyo.com • 01 47 23 54 01 • Admission: €6**
**Tuesday-Sunday 12 am-12 pm. Closed January 1st , May 1st, and December 25th.**

Bare concrete floors, wire netting walls, loose cable dangling from the ceiling... This palace is no Versailles. But it does devote 7,700 square meters of space to the exhibition of the wildest new ideas in the visual arts, in a city where the heritage of the past has been known to stifle enthusiasm (read "funding") for the new and spontaneous. The huge empty spaces are a bonanza for emergent artists struggling for visibility. This is no place for an aristocratic perception of art, because the Palace aims to welcome the largest audience - even kids have their own "Tok tok" activities (Reservations: 01 47 23 35 16).

## Blockbusters: a must!

Like all important cities, Paris is the ideal place for visiting large, ambitious temporary shows. And, invariably, blockbuster shows attract huge crowds. Make your own visit more enjoyable by booking it ahead of time. You can buy tickets online from the Fnac bookstore chain at www.fnac.com. Click on the "Spectacles" tab, then "Musée-Exposition" in the list on the left. You will then reserve a date and time – an appointment to see the show – paying for the ticket with your credit card. Next, go to any Fnac store (there are five in Paris, at the Forum des Halles, Bastille, Montparnasse, Saint-Lazare, Place d'Italie, and Ternes) to pick up your tickets with the credit card you used to buy them and a form of ID. No endless waiting in line!

## Musée Galliera
FASHION

**10 Avenue Pierre-Ier-de-Serbie, 16th • M° Iéna or Alma-Marceau**
**01 56 52 86 00. Admission: €7**
**Temporary exhibitions only; phone for information**
**Tuesday-Saturday 10 am-6 pm**

Just across the avenue from the Palais de Tokyo stands the fashion museum of Paris: thank God our city has one! Only open for special exhibitions, the museum, housed in an adorable 19th-century mansion surrounded by a garden, is assigned the duty of protecting more than 90,000 garments and costumes dating back to the 18th century. It draws on the collection to present themed shows focusing on specific decades, accessories, or innovative designers. Yves Saint-Laurent, Jean-Paul Gaultier, Balenciaga, and Christian Dior have all had this honor.

## Cité de l'Architecture et du Patrimoine
ARCHITECTURE THEN AND NOW

**1 Place du Trocadéro-et-du-Onze-Novembre, 16th • M° Trocadéro**
**www.citechaillot.fr • 01 58 51 52 00 • Admission: €8-10**
**Daily (except Tuesday) 11 am-7 pm; Thursday to 9 pm**
**Closed January 1st, May 1st, and December 25th**

Opened in 2007, the Cité de l'Architecture et du Patrimoine is a journey through French architecture from the Middle Ages to contemporary times. This institution is housed in the Palais de Chaillot, a monumental edifice built for the Universal Exhibition of 1937, located on the place du Trocadéro just across from the Eiffel Tower. This neighboring monument is as omnipresent in the museum as it is in the city: incredible views of the 7th, 15th and 16th arrondissements provide insight into Paris's urban system. The ground floor covers the Middle Ages to the 18th century, with copies of sculptures and mural and ceiling decorations, as well as scale models introducing the visitor to France's architectural treasures. The upper floor guides you through the 19th century to today, address-
ing the issues raised by the era of industry, the need for afford-able housing (with a reconstruc-tion of an apartment by Le Corbusier), and the amazing adventure of modern architec-ture. It's a thrilling presentation, with photo and video archives in addition to the model buildings. A great place for children, too, with a bookshop and a café.

## Musée Guimet
ASIAN ART

**6 Place d'Iéna, 16th • M° Iéna**
**www.guimet.fr • 01 56 52 53 00 • Admission to the permanent collections is free;**
**€7 for temporary exhibits • Daily (except Tuesday) 10 am-6 pm**

One of the unknown jewels of Paris, the Guimet Museum is dedicated to ancient Asian art: China, Japan, India, Pakistan, Korea, the Himalayas, and more... Galleries of statuary, monumental Buddhas, and priceless silks and brocades are on display, but the building itself, with its terracotta facade, is worthy of attention. The bodhisattvas and mandalas in the collection housed in the unique Panthéon Bouddhique (an annex at 19 Avenue d'Iéna) are likely to cast a meditative spell on you. A tiny Japanese garden is also hidden there.

## Musée Dapper
AFRICAN ART

**35 Rue Paul-Valéry, 16th • M° Victor-Hugo**
**www.dapper.com.fr • 01 45 00 91 75 • Admission: €6-9**
**Daily (except Tuesday) 11 am-7 pm**

This private foundation houses a fine collection of traditional African masks and sculpture. However, African music, dance, theater, and film are also showcased here. Themed shows (twice a year) present the art and culture of ethnic groups from sub-Saharan Africa (the Dogon of Mali, the Yoruba of Nigeria) and of the communities which arose from the African diaspora in the New World: North and South America and the Caribbean. The museum is intimate and original.

# Architectural walk in the 16th arrondissement

At every dinner party you attend, bring the conversation around to your **architectural walk** through the 16th arrondissement, an area which, in addition to being classy, provides a view of vast array of 19th- and 20th-century trends in architecture and city planning. Very specific, therefore extremely chic.

**• Rue Mallet-Stevens, 16th • M° Ranelagh or Jasmin**
A whole street designed by Robert Mallet-Stevens, a French architect who was a major influence on architecture in the 1920s and 30s.
The six houses he designed for this small dead-end street are the essence of harmony in residential planning. Minimalism was his watchword, and the simplicity and unity of the whole, highlighted by tasteful Art Deco details, will delight lovers of architecture.

**• Fondation Le Corbusier • 8-10 square du Docteur-Blanche, 16th**
**M° Ranelagh or Jasmin**
**www.fondationlecorbusier.asso.fr • 01 42 88 75 72**
**Monday 1:30-6 pm; Tuesday-Thursday 10 am-12:30 pm and 1:30-6 pm;**
**Saturday 10 am-5 pm**
The great architect Le Corbusier designed these two villas, La Roche and Jeanneret, in the early 1920s, when he was developing his Purist esthetic. You can tour Villa La Roche, which epitomizes the artist's vision. Le Corbusier once said, "A house is a machine for living in," and by the time you complete the tour, you'll be a convert to his modernism.

# Shopping
# Bling Bling

A gold Rolex, oodles of silks, satins, and furs from Versace, bleached blond hair clipped like Victoria Beckham's: in short, a dollop of conspicuous consumption, a dash of ostentation, and an almost total absence of intellect. Mix it all together and you get that little "Bling Bling" that echoes in the ears of the tasteful. The flash of bling is especially common at certain hours on Avenue Montaigne. Wear your shades, or you're liable to be blinded by the sight of the platinum blond wives of Russian millionaires, spending fortunes on spike heels, designer bags, and other accessories no self-respecting fashion victim would dream of doing without. You'll have a ball watching these creatures, who sometimes seem to be from another planet, crossing from one sidewalk to the other (and not always simply to shop, in fact). Oddly enough, the US hip hop expression "Bling Bling" found its way into middle-class French lingo to describe the somewhat unorthodox tastes of the country's top rapper, Nicolas Sarkozy.

So, don your flip-flops (Havaianas, perhaps?) and stroll down fancy **Avenue Montaigne**, the Rodeo Drive of Paris. All the couture brands have stores here - Chanel, Dior, Azzaro, etc., convenient to the Plaza Athénée luxury hotel, where the Russian oligarchs and Saudi millionaires stay when they come to Paris for a shopping trip. It almost feels like London or New York, the way the bay-windowed mansions overlook the tree-lined street. There's big money in the air, and that's quite exotic!

Avenue Montaigne, 8th • M° Franklin-D.-Roosevelt or Alma-Marceau

 **Icon:** Cécilia ex-Sarkozy

## + What's the secret of Parisian style?

Do Parisians have personal shopping consultants? Perhaps it has something to do with urban attitude, or the quality of European brands... That's only part of the solution, and the other part is within your reach, once you understand it. For Parisians, the way to find your style is to be comfortable with yourself: what you wear or the way you live give you a unique fashion identity... so just be yourself! Parisian style is about combination: a savvy mixture of colors and textures creates the look. No outfit is the outfit! Wearing designer jeans with H&M tops and vintage cardigans reflects the need to be different and make a statement about yourself.
That's why we encourage you to wander around a variety of shopping itineraries, picking up new basics, ideas, or unusual accessories to create your own style. That's the Parisian process.
Official sales in January and July: great deals!

## Soixante-Six Champs-Élysées

FASHION CONCEPT STORE (WOMEN/MEN)

**66 Avenue des Champs-Élysées, 8th**
**www.le66.fr • 01 53 53 33 80**
**Monday-Friday 11 am-8:30 pm; Saturday 11:30 am-8:3 pm; Sunday 2:30-7:30 pm**

This modern and unusual four-floor mall is a 12,000-square-foot paean to minimalism, the perfect formula for emphasizing the brand-name merchandise on sale. You'll find a sportswear and fashion arcade, a bookstore, a Potemkin DVD store, and a drugstore. Far more daring than the surrounding shops, it's also the place to go for special, limited-edition photographs and magazines.

## L'Éclaireur

FASHION CONCEPT STORE (WOMEN/MEN)

**8 Rue Boissy-d'Anglas, 8th • M° Concorde • 01 53 43 03 70**
**26 Avenue des Champs-Élysées, 8th • M° Champs-Élysées • 01 45 62 12 32**
**And also:**
**10 Rue Hérold, 1st • M° Bourse • 01 40 41 09 89**
**3 ter Rue des Rosiers, 4th • M° Saint-Paul • 01 48 87 10 22**
**12 Rue Malher, 4th • M° Saint-Paul • 01 44 54 22 11**

State-of-the-art creative research is on display in the boutiques run by Armand and Martine Hadida. They have always aimed for the top of the market, while discriminating carefully between mere high-ticket flamboyance and true luxury. For example, you'll find clothes by Thomas Wylde and Oscar de la Renta, Rosa Marie rings, Robert Wan black pearls, and more. If you only have time to visit one of the shops, choose the flagship store on Rue Boissy-d'Anglas. Splendid!

## Galerie Mouvements Modernes

DESIGNART

**112-114 Rue La Boétie, 8th**
**www.mouvementsmodernes.com • 01 45 08 08 82**
**Tuesday-Friday 11 am-7 pm; Saturday by appointment**

A paradise for design lovers, and a magnet attracting collectors from around the world, Mouvements Modernes was assembled in 2002 by Pierre Staudenmeyer, a highly respected scholar of the decorative arts. In September 2008, the gallery moved to a beautiful space in the heart of the Golden Triangle, the chic neighborhood near the Champs-Élysées. Mouvements Modernes focuses on dozens of postwar artists and designers exploring the fine line between art, design, and architecture. If you want to invest in design, this is the place!

# 6.

# Batignolles, Montmartre and Pigalle

Your first time around, you probably admired the Sacré-Cœur Basilica at the top of Montmartre hill, and cringed at the sex shops lining the boulevard lined at Pigalle. (Or vice-versa?) It's a good thing that's over with, because there's so much to explore on this hill, the second time around: adorable streets and squares, a lively village atmosphere, fledgling designers, and trendy nightlife. It's a vibrant part of Paris.

# Parisians' Secret Eateries

## Le Bistrot des Dames
FRENCH ◆

**18 Rue des Dames, 17th • M° Place-de-Clichy • 01 45 22 13 42 (no reservation)**
**Daily Monday-Friday 12-2:30 pm and 7 pm-2 am; Saturday and Sunday 12 pm-2 am**

Quite the institution on the Rue des Dames! Traditional fulfilling French menu, great wine list (our personal favorite: a glass of divine red Coulanges) and an old-movie interior. If the weather is fine, and if you can get there early, and if you're lucky (many ifs are involved), we strongly suggest you request a table in the garden. This simple bistro soirée could turn out to be one of the most romantic souvenirs in your Parisian scrapbook.

## Fuxia
ITALIAN ◆

**69 Place du Docteur-Félix-Lobligeois, 17th**
**M° Rome**
**www.fuxia.fr • 01 42 28 07 79 • Daily 9 am-12 am**

Fuxia (rhymes with "fuschia") serves up its delicious, simple fare in the Batignolles neighborhood, right next to the church on the area's most villagelike square. In the summertime, you can even eat al fresco and watch the kids at play... The restaurant does not take reservations, so come early or be patient (you can put your name on a list). Choose the pasta of the day or try the salads and bruschettas, always fresh and colorful. If you can't finish the bottle of wine you ordered, they'll only charge you for what you drank. A well-stocked "gelateria" will gladden diners with a sweet tooth.

## Les Puces des Batignolles
FRENCH ◆◆

**110 Rue Legendre, 17th • M° La Fourche or Brochant • 01 42 26 62 26**
**Daily 7:30 am-12 am**

A cosy address in the quiet Batignolles area, Les Puces gets its name from its flea-market décor, a jumble of old-fashioned French curios. The food is top-notch: luscious meats (entrecôte, ribs), seafood with crunchy vegetables, and over-the-top desserts (splurge on the Nutella Tiramisu!), all attractively presented on unmatched china. The service is young and friendly. An excellent choice for a dinner for two.

## Wassana
THAÏ ◆

**10 Rue Ganneron, 18th • M° La Fourche or Place-de-Clichy • 01 44 70 08 54**
**Daily 12-2:30 pm and 7-10:30 pm; closed for lunch Saturdays and Sundays**

Hold it right there! You are about to enter one of the best Thai restaurants in Paris, as word of mouth puts it. Located in a quiet street behind the busy Place de Clichy, it offers fine, delicate tradi-tional dishes in a suave, candlelit setting. Be aware that your palate might not be prepared for the heat of some of the dishes: when you order, let the chef know about your tolerance for chili pepper!

## Brasserie Wepler
FRENCH ◆

**14 Place de Clichy, 18th • M° Place-de-Clichy**
**www.wepler.com • 01 45 22 53 24**
**Daily until 1 am**

The Wepler is a venerable refuge from the noisy traffic and bustling sidewalks of the Place de Clichy: a spacious, quiet, old-fash-ioned brasserie with white tablecloths, which has changed little since Édouard Vuillard painted it in 1910. It has become a hangout for movie-business folk and therefore film-lovers. All ages and nation-alities fill the place, drinking beers from the tap or sipping wine. The supper crowd is a bit more fashion-conscious.

## L'Aubergine
FRENCH ◆◆

**46 Rue des Dames, 17th • M° Place-de-Clichy**
**Monday-Saturday 11:30 am-3:30 pm and 6 pm-2 am**

Naturally, eggplant is on the menu at the Aubergine, although the word is also a synonym for meter maid, dating back to the days when they wore deep-purple uniforms (they've been in periwinkle blue since the 80s, at least). This Batignolles restaurant, one of our favorite hangouts in the neighborhood, also serves, a fine beef tartare and rosemary chicken, and if you ask for Pierre and Fabien, you might get a free orgasme (one of the house's special cocktails).

# Chéri Bibi
FRENCH FUSION ◆ ◆

**15 Rue André-del-Sarte, 18th • M° Anvers or Barbès-Rochechouart**
**01 42 54 88 96**
**Monday-Saturday 8-11 pm**

With its vintage Fifties interior, smiling waitresses, and jocular crowd, it looks like your average trendy restaurant. The difference is that the menu here is cooked lovingly, with a grandmother's touch, and features the classic French comfort foods: rillettes, boeuf bourguignon. Unlike your grandmother, perhaps, the chef also knows how to peel a mango... Hurry! Chéri Bibi is a rising star.

# Osteria Ascolani
ITALIAN ◆

**98 Rue des Martyrs, 18th • M° Pigalle or Abbesses**
**www.osteria-ascolani.com • 01 42 62 43 94**
**Nightly, 7 pm-2 am; Friday, Saturday, Sunday, and holidays lunch is also served**

The setting is simple, the owners genuine Italians, and the food superb in this cantina, one of the best restaurants in the neighborhood. Locals don't even check the "daily special" before going in: great taste is guaranteed. Helpings are generous, so be mindful you must save room for the panna cotta dessert...it's heavenly!

# Le Floors
AMERICAN ◆ ◆

**100 Rue Myrha, 18th • M° Château-Rouge • 01 42 62 08 08**
**Tuesday-Friday 9-2 am; Saturday-Sunday 10-2 am**

In an impressive-looking, spanking-new, three-story glass structure - a former print shop - in a neighborhood on the edge of the Goutte d'Or, gradually gentrifying, just over the boundary from the foothills of Montmartre. Recently opened to the joy of local, this "American-style" diner offers a creative selection of burgers. Try the Japanese-inspired one, quite a surprise.

My addresses around Batignolles, Montmartre and Pigalle

# Georgette
FRENCH ◆◆

**29 Rue Saint-Georges, 9th • M° Notre-Dame-de-Lorette
01 42 80 39 13
Tuesday-Friday 12-2:15 pm and 7:30-10 pm**

Madame Georgette is one of those typically Parisian ladies whose consummate skill you never tire of admiring, as she juggles dish towels and glasses behind the counter... She is the soul of this French restaurant just south of Place Saint-Georges. The place has the  charm of the Fifties, with black-and-white tiles and dulling mirrors. The food is classical French bistro style, with starters like leeks vinaigrette or a hard-boiled egg, potted duck or fresh fish to follow, and crème caramel to finish. 100% authentic.

# Le Restaurant
FRENCH ◆◆

**32 Rue Véron, 18th • M° Blanche
www.lerestaurant.fr • 01 42 23 06 22
Daily 12-2:30 pm and 7:30-11:30 pm**

Located in a quiet street off the Rue Lepic, a block below the Rue des Abbesses, "Le Restaurant" offers traditional French cuisine in a beautiful setting with lofty stone walls.

# No Stress Café
WORLD ◆

**24 Rue Clauzel, on the place Gustave-Toudouze, 9th
M° Saint-Georges • 01 48 78 00 27
Tuesday-Sunday 10-1 am**

Look for the row of restaurants on the pleasant, tree-lined square. This one is famous for its Sunday brunch, scrumptious cheeseburgers, wok platters, and... palm reading!

## Pizza war!

**La Pizzetta** ◆
**20 Avenue Trudaine, 9th • M° Pigalle**
**www.lapizzetta.fr • 01 48 78 14 08**
**Monday-Saturday 12:30-2:30 pm**
**and 7:30-11 pm; open for lunch Sundays**

With its high white ceilings and black-and-white photos hanging on the walls, this pizzeria owes something to Manhattan's Little Italy. There the resemblance ends, however, for the pizza features such unusual toppings as asparagus cream or arugula. An added plus: saffron and whole-wheat crusts are offered, in addition to the usual white. Delicioso!

**Pizzeria Da Carmine** ◆
**61 Rue des Martyrs, 9th • M° Pigalle**
**01 48 78 28 01**
**Tuesday-Saturday 5 pm-12 am**

The second contender for the title: you'll undoubtedly have to wait a bit, but it's worth it! An ultra-Italian ambience, very busy, and quite loud when an Italian soccer match is airing on the wall-mounted TV. It's time to remember your Italian, and try a " buena sera," a "grazie"... perhaps even a "caro"? You'll feel like kissing the chef, the pizza is so good. Our personal favorite: the pizza with porcini and arugula. Don't mention dessert; you'll be full...

## Delmontel vs Bakery ✚

The toughest choice in Pigalle: buying your pastries at Arnaud Delmontel, the Sarkozys' favorite, or at the trendy British spot, Rose Bakery.

**Rose Bakery: 46 Rue des Martyrs, 9th**
**M° Pigalle or Anvers**

**Arnaud Delmontel: 39 Rue des Martyrs, 9th**
**M° Pigalle or Anvers**

# The Night Time
## is the Right Time

The nightlife is eclectic, going from the floor show at the Moulin Rouge, home of the can-can and a mandatory stop on the package-tour circuit, to up-to-the-minute music halls and the performers who strum guitars at neighborhood bars in the Rue des Abbesses or the Batignolles area.

## Les Caves Populaires

DRINKS

**22 Rue des Dames, 17th • M° Place-de-Clichy**
**www.cavespopulaires.com • 01 53 04 08 32**
**Daily 8-2 am**

The Batignolles area is not especially hospitable to the party animal, who is expected to head for Pigalle and let honest folk sleep. Thank God for Les Caves Populaires! You'll be surrounded by with artsy musicians and laid-back fashion victims... It's always crowded, but that's part of the fun. The waitstaff are friendly, and open to any questions, especially if you're in a wine-tasting mood. Feel free to mingle!

## Café Burq

DRINKS

**6 Rue Burq, 18th • M° Abbesses**
**01 42 52 81 27**
**Monday-Saturday 6 pm-2 am**

Café Burq is a folksy, hip restaurant and bar. The dinner quality-price ratio leaves something to be desired, but after 10 pm, it becomes a favorite neighborhood hangout for drinks. You simply cannot go there without trying the special house cocktail, "Chien Hurlant" (Howling Dog). The crowd is trendy, talkative, and fun, especially after they've downed a few of these vodka-strawberry-Tabasco delights...

## Le Soleil de la Butte
DRINKS & DANCING

**32 Rue Muller, 18th • M° Château-Rouge • 01 46 06 18 24**
**Monday-Thursday and Sunday 9 am-2 am; Friday and Saturday 10 pm-6 am**

From the street, it looks like a simple brasserie, serving salads and omelettes. But when night falls, it turns into a frenetic little club. A multifarious crowd of locals boogies all night long to jazz and modern tunes. One of the best-kept secrets of the Butte Montmartre...

## La Chope du Château Rouge
DRINKS

**40 Rue de Clignancourt, 18th • M° Barbès-Rochechouart**
**01 46 06 20 10 • Daily 7-2 am**

This is the kind of bar we love, casual and friendly, a fixture that looks like it's always been there. Grab a beer, meet friends, listen to soft music... Life. The owners offer a couscous dinner on Friday and Saturday nights. On the road again!

## Les Noctambules
DRINKS

**24 Boulevard de Clichy, 18th • M° Pigalle**
**01 46 06 16 38 • Nightly 10:30 pm-4:30 am**

A Pigalle landmark. It's almost impossible to describe the ambience of this cheerful yet lonesome bar, open all night long, where you might encounter the most surprising people. The stupendous Pierre Carré, warbling popular French melodies from the 30s and 40s to the tinkling sound of a piano-and-drum ensemble, is so retro-camp with his Elvis pompadour and red suit, you'll think you're hallucinating...

## Au rendez-vous des amis
DRINKS

**23 Rue Gabrielle, 18th • M° Abbesses or Pigalle • Daily 8:30-2 am**

It truly is a gathering place for friends, though they must climb the cobble-stoned hill to reach it. In fact, it may be the highest-altitude bar in the city. Nevertheless, it's a hospitable roof where you can browse the newspaper, enjoy a glass of rosé, or snack on a plate of cheeses, just enjoying the groove. It hosts many events, such as concerts, readings, and exhibits of all sorts.

## Chez Ginette
DRINKS

**101 Rue Caulaincourt, 18th • M° Lamarck-Caulaincourt**
**www.chez-ginette.com • 01 46 06 01 49**
**Daily 9 am-2 am; serving food non-stop 12 pm-12 am**

On the northern side of the Butte Montmartre, the downward slope of the roller-coaster, you'll hit Rue Caulaincourt, a charming avenue lined with trees and beautiful buildings. It's very residential, but wherever there are Parisians, there's a café! Chez Ginette even has a terrace to offer....

## Le Divan du Monde
DRINKS & LIVE MUSIC

**75 Rue des Martyrs, 18th • M° Pigalle or Anvers**
**www.divandumonde.com • 01 40 05 06 99**

The Divan is almost always hopping with live music: festivals, parties, happy hours (their version starts at 7 and lasts until 11 pm!), often with no cover charge. The focus is on jazz and world music, with a smattering of electro. The easygoing, open-minded crowd asks for nothing more than a great party. Back when Toulouse-Lautrec used to sketch here, it was the Divan Japonais, but now it's gone even more international.

## La Fourmi
DRINKS

**74 Rue des Martyrs, 18th • M° Pigalle or Anvers**
**01 42 64 70 35**
**Monday-Thursday 8-2 am; Friday-Saturday 8-4 am; Sunday 10-2 am**

Buzzing practically 'round the clock, La Fourmi (literally, "the ant") is a Pigalle institution, always brimming with that trendy arty crowd that we love! Should you be thirsty, it's ideal for a drink before crossing the street to the Divan du Monde, or walking down to La Cigale (the grasshopper of the fable) for live music and concerts. And when the sun finally shines on Paris again, after one of those long rainy spells, its sidewalk tables receive maximal rays.

## Chez Moune
DRINKS & DANCING

**54 Rue Pigalle, 9th • M° Pigalle**
**www.chez-moune.com • 01 45 26 64 64**
**Tuesday-Saturday from 10:30 pm**

A team of outrageously fashionable people has been buying up old night-clubs and bringing them back to life, in all their kitschy splendor. Chez Moune, founded as a lesbian cabaret in 1936, is the latest to get a new coat of paint-purple, naturally. It's just one of a string of venues to take off like a rocket after a minimal makeover, a few of the others being Hôtel Amour, Paris-Paris, or Le Baron. Beware: it's especially hard to get in.

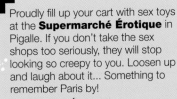

Proudly fill up your cart with sex toys at the **Supermarché Érotique** in Pigalle. If you don't take the sex shops too seriously, they will stop looking so creepy to you. Loosen up and laugh about it... Something to remember Paris by!

**Supermarché Érotique:**
**76 Boulevard de Clichy, 18th**
**M° Blanche**

## Le Kitch'Up
DRINKS & LIVE MUSIC

**39 Boulevard de Clichy, 9th • M° Blanche**
**www.kitchup.blogspot.com**
**Tuesday-Saturday 7 pm-6 am**

The Kitch'Up is not easy to find. It is located on the second floor, above of one of the many Irish pubs that line the boulevard heading west from Le Moulin Rouge. But now that you're in on the secret, climb the stairs, and dance until dawn to the sound of an unknown DJ talent. The motley crowd makes this kitschy, homey place the trendiest bar in the neighborhood.

My addresses around Batignolles, Montmartre and Pigalle

# Culture Mix

Montmartre is famous as the cradle of Impressionist art, in the 19th century, when Auguste Renoir and Toulouse-Lautrec roamed the cabarets, and in the early 20th century, Picasso settled at the Bâteau-Lavoir, on Place Emile-Goudeau. Suzanne Valadon raised her son Maurice Utrillo at the top of the Butte. Their presence still haunts the quieter streets. Wander away from the main tourist drag, and discover that romance will always be part of Paris.

## Musée de la Vie Romantique
ROMANTICISM & WONDERFUL GARDEN

**Hôtel Scheffer-Renan • 16 Rue Chaptal, 9th • M° Saint-Georges**
**01 55 31 95 67 • Admission to the permanent collection is free; it varies for temporary exhibits**
**Tuesday-Sunday 10 am-6 pm**

In the 1830s, French romanticism was in its heyday, and successful novelist George Sand (the pseudonym of feminist Aurore Dupin) settled in this neighborhood with her consumptive exiled Polish genius-composer-pianist lover, Frédéric Chopin. (Outdo that for romance!) This particular dwelling, the home of their friend the painter Ary Scheffer, is filled with Sand memorabilia. The mansion's small garden, where a *salon de thé* dispenses steaming pots of the stuff, along with homemade cakes, is enchanting.

# ✚Just have a look!

### Rue Frochot, 9th • M° Pigalle

On the northeastern side of the intersection between Rues Frochot, Henry-Monnier, and Victor-Massé, you will bump into the gateway to a private residential street. On the façade of one of the buildings, behold the sublime Art Déco stained-glass interpretation of a landscape by the Japanese artist Hokusaï. Ever eclectic, Montmartre!

### Place Saint-Georges, 9th • M° Saint-Georges

One of the jewels of the 9th arrondissement, a short walk down from Pigalle and its busy streets. The middle of the square is adorned with a bust of the French illustrator Paul Gavarni, with bas-relief Pierrot harlequins dancing around the pedestal. The 19th-century courtesan (or *grande horizontale*) Blanche de la Païva lived in the ornate townhouse at n° 28, and French statesman Adolphe Thiers at n° 27.

## Musée de Montmartre

LA BOHÈME!

**12 Rue Cortot, 18th • M° Lamarck-Caulaincourt**
**www.museedemontmartre.fr • 01 46 06 61 11**
**Tuesday-Sunday 10 am-12:30 pm and 1:30-6 pm • Admission: €4.50**

Since 1960, the oldest house on the hill, surrounded by a charming garden, has been the Montmartre Museum. The mansion once belonged to the actor Rosimond (1640-1686), one of the first Sociétaires of the Comédie-Française. Some two centuries later, the house commons were converted to artists' studios, which were rented to a number of illustrious painters. This is where

Auguste Renoir worked on his large canvas *Le Bal du Moulin de la Galette*; Suzanne Valadon, Maximilien Luce, Maurice Utrillo, Federico Zandomeneghi, and Raoul Dufy were also tenants here on Rue Cortot.

The museum collection illustrates the neighborhood's history and days of glory, from the Abbey of the Dames de Montmartre to the golden age of the cabarets and devil-may-care Bohemian lifestyles, without omitting the red flags and revolutionary fervor of the 1871 Commune.

# ✚ Stroll through an early Montmartre morning!

• Begin on the northern slope of the hill, at Métro Lamarck-Caulaincourt, and climb the stairs to reach Rue Caulaincourt. Then wend your way along Avenue Junot, with its Art Deco studio-dwellings. Keep your eyes peeled for Villa Léandre, the rosy brick homes at 23 bis; then turn left on Rue Simon-Dereure, which will lead you to the Allée des Brouillards and its castle. When you reach Rue Girardon, turn right, and your eyes will behold the Moulin de la Galette, which once housed a dance hall immortalized by Renoir in the late 19th century.

• Go back up Rue Girardon, retracing your steps, until you hit Rue de l'Abreuvoir, on the right. Then take another right on Rue des Saules, where you'll see the little pink cottage housing the Lapin Agile at 22. This is where painters and poets used to carouse, far into the night. Rue Saint-Vincent will then take you to the peak of the Rue du Mont-Cenis and Rue du Chevalier-de-la-Barre (follow it to the top, to explore its romantic stairs and the view of Paris). Soon you will reach Saint-Pierre de Montmartre church, one of the oldest in Paris. It is dwarfed by its neighbor, the basilica of Sacré-Cœur (open 9 am-6 pm, to 1 am in the summertime), edified in 1873 "to expiate the crimes of the Commune." Its dome offers a beautiful panorama of Paris (admission: €5).

• After admiring the spectacular view from the piazza in front of the church, follow Rue Azaïs to the tourist-trappy Place du Tertre. Flee via Rue Norvins, Place Jean-Baptiste Clément, Rue de la Mire, and Rue Ravignan, which opens onto the tree-shaded cobblestones of Place Émile-Goudeau. The Bateau-Lavoir studios were located at 13. They housed many a young, penniless artist at the turn of the century. In fact, this is where Picasso painted *Les Demoiselles d'Avignon*.

• End your stroll by going downhill to the Rue des Abbesses. For dessert, turn left, cross the square, and follow Rue des Trois-Frères: the grocery store is the one in the film *Amélie Poulain*. As for the unforgettable Café des Deux Moulins, it is located to the west, at 15 Rue Lepic.

# La Cigale
LIVE MUSIC

**120 Boulevard de Rochechouart, 18th • M° Anvers or Pigalle**
**www.lacigale.fr • 01 49 25 81 75**

Named for the insect who fiddles the summer away while the ant is hard at work, La Cigale is a medium-sized concert hall. Smells like avant-garde! The theater was built in 1887, and such famous names in French song as Maurice Chevalier and Mistinguett have wowed audiences from this stage. In its sorriest years, in the 1970s, it was a movie house specializing in kung-fu films... In 1987, the venue was renovated by designer Philippe Starck and became one of the hotspots of the music scene, French and international. It's one of the best places to enjoy a singer's performance: magical moments of musical communion take place at La Cigale, and after the concert you can jabber about it to your heart's content down the sidewalk at La Fourmi, a great bar filled with musicians. Next door is La Boule Noire, La Cigale's sister club: the ambience is cozier and unplugged. Many concerts have open seating, so make sure to come early to snag the best seats!

## The Place to Be: Les Abbesses

This is Paris's ultimate hipster street. It has been dissed as a bit over-the-top, but don't listen to the naysayers! The unofficial southern boundary of Montmartre is lined with cafés, bookstores, boutiques, delis, bakeries, cheeseries, etc. The narrow up-and-down streets of the neighborhood are fun to explore.

**Around Rue des Abbesses, 18th**
**M° Abbesses**

## Studio 28
HISTORICAL MOVIE THEATER

**10 Rue Tholozé, 18th • M° Blanche**
**www.cinemastudio28.com • 01 46 06 36 07**

When it opened in 1928 with a screening of Napoléon by Abel Gance, Studio 28 was the first movie theater on the Butte Montmartre, and the nerve center of visionary cinema. It hosted the première of Luis Buñuel's Age d'Or in 1930. The theater has maintained its artistic integrity, and today it is the local art house. At the café tables in its small garden, you can have a drink and discuss movies with friends or strangers in the usual passionate French way! It's so typical, it has a cameo in Amélie Poulain.

## Cinéma des Cinéastes
INDEPENDENT MOVIES

**7 Avenue de Clichy, 17th • M° Place-de-Clichy**
**www.cinema-des-cineastes.fr • 08 926 897 17 • Admission: €8.70**

It's not just hype: the Cineastes' cinema really does attract filmmakers, hosting frequent premiere screenings. This is a theater with a soul, light years away from the multiplexes packing in the crowds for crass Hollywood blockbusters. Independent films from around the world are featured, in their original language. No commercials, no popcorn, but heavy discussions and intense emotions. A wine bar upstairs welcomes lovers of the 7th Art.

# ✚Young French singers

"Quand il me prend dans ses bras, je vois la vie en rose..." Édith Piaf is only one of the French singers and songwriters who are loved around the world. Charles Aznavour, Jean Ferrat, Juliette Gréco, Yves Montand and, more recently, Jean-Jacques Goldman and Alain Souchon, are pillars of French culture, resisting a global tide of bland musical sameness. The new millennium saw a new crop of vocalists mature. They have a fresh way of singing, making tender, funny poetry out of everyday life. Let's applaud Vincent Delerm, M (Mathieu Chédid), Bénabar, Cali, Daniel Darc, Renan Luce. Now it's the ladies' turn: Camille, Daphné, Keren Ann, Juliette, Olivia Ruiz, Pauline Croze, etc.

**They sing their hearts out at the Bataclan, La Cigale, La Boule Noire, the Olympia... And more:**

**• Le Nouveau Casino:**
**109 Rue Oberkampf, 11th**
**M° Saint-Maur or Oberkampf**
**www.nouveaucasino.net**

**• La Maroquinerie:**
**23 Rue Boyer, 20th**
**M° Ménilmontant**
**www.lamaroquinerie.fr**

**• L'Européen:**
**5 Rue Biot, 17th**
**M° Place-de-Clichy**
**www.leuropeen.info**

My addresses around Batignolles, Montmartre and Pigalle

# Shopping
# Vintage Chic

**D**on't be fooled by the hordes of souvenir merchants and sex shops. The area south of Montmartre is one of the funkiest, most joyful villages in Paris, and one of our personal favorites for shopping. Walking around the cobblestone streets, you might just come across that perfect accessory or vintage object to make you feel like a Parisian "bobo" ("Bohemian Bourgeois").

 **Icon:** Audrey Tautou, actress

### Guerrisol
SECOND HAND CLOTHES

**29 and 67 Avenue de Clichy, 17th • M° Place-de-Clichy**
**Monday-Saturday 10 am-7 pm**

African families and fashion addicts alike are drawn to this second-hand emporium, where you rummage through the bins and racks and often find treasure at an unbeatably low price. No two garments are alike: it's strictly the luck of the catch. Great for leather coats, vintage trench coats, seventies boots, and granny's pocketbooks...
*Bag (from €15) / Shirt (from €2) / Leather jacket (from €15)*

## Ubé Ulé
FASHION (WOMEN/CHILDREN)

**59 Rue Condorcet, 9th • M° Pigalle or Anvers**
**Tuesday-Saturday 9:30 am-7 pm**

Rue Condorcet offers a good choice for kids and baby stuff. But, girls, entering Ubé Ulé is like opening the door to your fantasy child's room: vintage furniture painted in intense pastels, a bazaar of clothes, bed covers, and soft toys. Most of the clothes are designed right in the store by their own talented stylists, using beautiful Liberty fabrics and vintage buttons. Future moms, take a look at their wonderful selection of "expecting" outfits as well.
*Liberty-print dress (€55-65) / Sarongs (€25)*

## Wochdom
VINTAGE FASHION (WOMEN/MEN)

**72 Rue Condorcet, 9th • M° Pigalle**
**Monday-Saturday 12-8 pm**

Hunting through a flea market in desperate search for a terrific vintage item takes hours. Well, now you don't have to. Just go to Wochdom for a selection of the trendiest vintage clothes, shoes and (OMG!) fabulous purses.
*Dress (€40) / Purse (€30) / Shoes (€30)*

## White Spirit
HOME

**30 Rue Henry-Monnier, 9th**
**M° Pigalle or Saint-Georges**
**Tuesday-Saturday 11 am-7:30 pm**

Inspired by fashion designer Martin Margiela's all white-ambience, the owner of this tiny yet homey shop selects furniture and lamps that are simple yet stylish. She loves mixing basic vintage furniture, painted white or black, heavy white dishware and crafty designer lamps made of rusted metal and white fabric.
*Poetic oversize white paper lamps (from €180). Stylish rusted metal candlestick (€20)*

## Et Puis C'est Tout !
HOME (VINTAGE)

**72 Rue des Martyrs, 9th • M° Pigalle**
**Tuesday-Saturday 12-7:30 pm; Monday 2-7 pm**

Don't let the grumpy owner fool you: he is an expert in restoring vintage (old-time) factory lamps. This address is a well-kept secret for 50s to 70s furniture at very good prices. You will also find treasures of French popular culture: take home a vintage pastis jug, a fifties poster, or a colorful vintage ashtray.
*Pastis jug (€10) / Poster (€3) / Ashtray (€15)*

My addresses around Batignolles, Montmartre and Pigalle

## Antoine et Lili
FASHION (WOMEN/CHILDREN)

**90 Rue des Martyrs, 18th • M° Abbesses or Pigalle**
**Monday-Friday 11 am-8 pm; Saturday 10:30 am-8 pm**
**Other addresses:**
- **3 Rue du Vingt-Neuf-Juillet, 1st • M° Tuileries**
- **17 Rue du Jour, 1st • M° Les Halles**
- **87 Rue de Seine, 6th • M° Odéon**
- **51 Rue des Francs-Bourgeois, 4th • M° Rambuteau**
- **95 Quai de Valmy, 10th • M° Jacques-Bonsergent**

You can't miss it. Bright pink, with the scent of incense floating out, Antoine et Lili is a Paris institution for offbeat clothes and accessories. Their collections are inspired by Eastern Europe and Asia, with blacks and bright colors, always exuberant, unabashedly bright. Also, choose from a big selection of miscellaneous accessories: anything from Chinese sequin shoes to metal plates that the creative owners bring back from their many travels.
*Necklace (€7) / Sweater (€65)*

## Homies
FASHION (WOMEN)

**42 Rue des Abbesses, 9th • M° Abbesses or Pigalle**
**Tuesday-Saturday 11 am-8 pm; Sunday 2-7:30 pm**

Why isn't fashion always this simple? A cheerful owner, a little dog, soft music, and a load of trendy and affordable must-haves. The selection mixes laid back but feminine clothes, creative lines, soft fabrics, and lots of cotton. If you're lucky, you might also find your size in top fashion shoes and belts.
*Dress (€70) / Shoes (€100)*

## Petit Bateau
FASHION (CHILDREN/WOMEN)

**50 Rue des Abbesses, 18th • M° Abbesses**
**Monday-Saturday 10 am-7 pm**

Petit Bateau began as a top quality brand of children's knit underclothing. From there, it was just a short step to making and marketing the fine cotton T-shirts in a range of colors and shapes that sell like hot cakes to women. Everyone has at least one Petit Bateau waiting for its day in the sun. The white T-shirt with the picot-edged neckline is a classic all year long.
*Infant's bodysuit (€7.70) / Short-sleeved T-shirt (from €10) and long sleeved (from €12)*

## Spree
FASHION (WOMEN), HOME & ART

**16 Rue de La Vieuville, 18th • M° Abbesses or Pigalle**
**Sunday-Monday 3-7 pm; Tuesday-Thursday 11 am-7:30 pm;**
**Friday-Saturday 10:30 am-7:30 pm; closed for lunch (1-2 pm)**

Who would have thought that a trendissima shop & gallery could be nestled in the heart of Montmartre? In a fabulous loft, a very creative couple has mixed together international style, art, and design in a surprisingly comfortable and welcoming atmosphere. Browse through their excellent selection of current designer collections (APC, Isabel Marrant, Marc Jacobs...), relish a photo exhibit, pick up an Eames chair or just go for inspiration...

*Pants (€180) / Blouse (€120)*

## Emmanuelle Zysman
FASHION & ACCESSORIES

**81 Rue des Martyrs, 18th • M° Abbesses**
**Tuesday-Friday 11 am-7 pm;**
**Saturday 12-8 pm; Sunday 3:30-7 pm**

Emmanuelle Zysman became famous in Paris with retro bags borrowing from colonial imagery with postcard appliqués. Today she stills creates handbags, but the focus is on jewelry: beautiful and discreet rings, necklaces, or bracelets, symbols of subtle Paris chic.

*Bag (from €90) / Jewelry (from €45)*

## Tatiana Lebedev
FASHION

**23 Rue Houdon, 18th • M° Abbesses**
**Tuesday-Saturday 11 am-7 pm; Sunday 2-7 pm**

A native Russian fashion designer, Tatiana Lebedev, proposes hand painted t-shirts, structured clothes, crumpled denim jackets, and reversible cotton skirts, for an unmistakable femnine look. Don't let the graphic modernity of the designs frighten you away: try something on. You may love the style on you.

*Dress (€100)*

# The wide world around the corner: Barbès-Rochechouart

This intersection, with the elevated Métro line, symbolizes the center of Paris's North and sub-Saharan immigrant communities. Not quite your chic venue, Barbès (two syllables: bar-besse) still has a wonderful atmosphere, full of life and overcrowded sidewalks. A few addresses define the place:

• **Tati: 18 Boulevard de Rochechouart, 18th • M° Barbès-Rochechouart**

Bargains galore! Tati clothes the masses from head to toe, casual to dressy - you can even find wedding dresses there! You'll have to comb through mountains of clothes, but you may find a treasure.

• **Marché Saint-Pierre, Reine and Moline: 2 Rue Charles-Nodier, 18th • M° Anvers**

The streets directly below Sacré-Coeur contain at least three big fabric stores, and dozens of smaller ones. The offer includes cottons, polyesters, silks, satins, woolens, fake furs, and even terrycloth, fluorescent nylon net, and mattress ticking. If you sew, you'll be engrossed in the bonanza of colors, textures, and possibilities. If you don't, look around and enjoy the mood. Seamstresses of every stripe peer at the bolts of fabric, from wealthy 16th-arrondissement housewives to African mamas and rising fashion designers.

# The pleasures of flea-market browsing

On spring and summer weekends, fleamarkets spring up on Parisian sidewalks, in the French version of the garage sale. Both amateur and professionals unload antiques and collectibles: posters, pastis pitchers, lamps, glasses, linens, books, games, toys...

Check the website **brocabrac.fr** for details and adresses (sorry, only in French, but Paris is "75").

Year-round, the professionals wheel and deal from their stalls in **Saint-Ouen** (Saturday to Monday, M° Porte-de-Clignancourt) or **Vanves** (Saturday and Sunday mornings, M° Porte-de-Vanves, 14th).

# 7.

# Canal Saint-Martin, République and La Villette

We're willing to bet you missed this area your fist time around. After decades of being superbly ignored by Parisians, real-estate values are on the rise in a neighborhood that includes such amenities as a quiet canal, little automobile traffic, and picturesque bridges. It has become one of the hotspots of the capital, famous for its underground nightlife, trendy shops, and uber-bobo inhabitants. Come discover another face of Paris...

# Parisians'
## Secret
# Eateries

## Le Cambodge

CAMBODIAN ◆

**10 Avenue Richerand, 10th • M° Jacques-Bonsergent**
**www.lecambodge.fr • 01 44 84 37 70 (no reservation)**
**Monday-Saturday 12-2:30 pm and 8-11:30 pm**

In this excellent traditional Cambodian diner, you need to arrive early, sometimes before it opens, and wait for your turn. But Parisians do it, because the food is worth the wait: the Bo-Bun (thinly sliced beef or pork, bean sprouts, cucumber, and fresh mint and cilantro on cold cooked rice noodles) is near perfection, fresh as can be, and the prices are very reasonable (€8 for the Bo-Bun, our absolute favorite).

## Ploum

JAPANESE ◆◆

**20 Rue Alibert, 10th • M° République or Goncourt**
**www.ploum.fr • 01 42 00 11 90**
**Monday-Friday 12-2 pm and 7-11 pm; Saturday and Sunday 7-11 pm**

Unlike the Hôtel du Nord above, Ploum is a hipster newcomer, drawn by the neighborhood's sudden recovery, surfing the sushi craze. But they do it with skill and style: the restful Zen-inspired interior, with booths and bare concrete floors, is brought to life by jovial chefs and an appreciative young crowd. In addition to the standards sushi and sashimi, they've added novelties like foie de lotte, liver of monkfish, an Atlantic Ocean species popular on French tables.

## Urbane

FRENCH ◆◆

**12 Rue Arthur-Groussier, 10th • M° Goncourt or Colonel-Fabien**
**www.myspace.com/urbaneparis • 01 42 40 74 75**
**Tuesday-Saturday for lunch and dinner. Brunch on Sunday**

Who said lunch had to be dull? For €15, you can thrill your senses with seared tuna on a bed of arugula, seasoned with balsamic vinegar, as a starter, and a beautiful salmon filet. Vintage furniture is set off well by the exposed stone walls and grey trim, but Urbane's main selling point is market-fresh ingredients and imaginative cuisine.

## Hôtel du Nord
FRENCH ◆◆

**102 Quai de Jemmapes, 10th • M° République or Jacques-Bonsergent**
**www.hoteldunord.org • 01 40 40 78 78**
**Daily 12-3 pm and 8 pm-12 am**

A legendary location, for which the 1938 Marcel Carné feature melo-drama, about a romantic suicide pact that goes awry, was named. The star Arletty immortalized the whole neighborhood with her scene on the bridge:"Atmosphèèèère, atmosphèèèrere, est-ce que j'ai une gueule d'atmo-sphère?"... Today, you can pay homage to the golden age of French movies in this very good and slightly trendy restaurant attracting Parisians of every age, style and - dare we say - class? The place to be on the Canal! Primavera pastas share the menu with osso-bucos and raw fish.
If Hôtel du Nord is crowded, try Le Poisson Rouge: 112 Quai de Jemmapes (www.le-poisson-rouge.com)

## Le Chateaubriand
FRENCH ◆◆

**129 Avenue Parmentier, 11th • M° Goncourt**
**01 43 57 45 95**
**Monday-Friday 12-2 pm and 8-9:30 pm; Saturday 8-9:30 pm**

Enchanting in every way. Basque chef Inaki Aizpitarte, a rising star, has introduced a modern, high-concept din-ner menu to the timeless bistro setting of Le Chateau-briand. The good-looking garçons, engaging and entertaining, don't put you off with the usual chilly Parisian professionalism. You'll be at ease in this typical eastern Paris hangout, which boasts an impressive wine list. Lunch offerings are more traditional, including boudin noir with apples and the Basque delight piperade.

## Le Réfectoire
FRENCH ◆◆

**80 Boulevard Richard-Lenoir, 11th • M° Oberkampf**
**01 48 06 74 85**
**Daily 12-2 pm and 8-11 pm**

You'll do a double-take when you see the playful Pop-Art interior, with over-sized lighting fixtures that Claes Oldenburg might have designed. The crowd from La Famille in the 18th had a ball when they moved in here. It's back to childhood, especially at dessert, with offerings like "Nutella crème brulée" or "Carambar mousse." The staff doesn't just serve: they really interact with their customers. Let yourself be spoiled rotten!

# The Night Time is the Right Time

Paris is no Berlin but this is our own little "underground" area offering sharp music in casual settings, the throbbing pulse of young, artsy Paris...

## Point Ephémère

DRINKS

**200 Quai de Valmy, 10th • M° Jaurès**
**www.pointephemere.org • 01 40 34 02 48**
**Daily 12 pm-2 am; brunch on Saturdays and Sundays**

Point Ephemere, a "center of artistic dynamics" funded by government grants, took over a 14,000-square-foot warehouse at the northwestern end of the canal. There's plenty of space for live concerts and shows, as well as studios for visual artists in residence and rehearsal space for performers. On a sunny day, you could laze away the whole afternoon at a picnic table on the dockside terrace, as one of the locals strums his guitar. And since this is France, the menu is fairly interesting, artistic, and dynamic as well.

## Le Café Chéri(e)

DRINKS

**44 Boulevard de la Villette, 19th • M° Belleville**
**www.cafecherie.blogspot.com • 01 42 02 02 05**
**Daily 8 am-2 pm. Music and DJ Thursday-Saturday 10 pm-2 am**

A magnet for hipsters on the Boulevard de la Villette, Café Chéri(e) features hip hop, electro, and funk music for your dancing pleasure, and cool, icy margaritas for your refreshment. Taking the love vibe to heart, the space is lit in red and graffiti-laden. The crowd that hangs out here is in its thirties (the fabulous thirties!) and really easygoing. At sunup, everyone sits on the sidewalk in a laidback way. Mismatched chairs and tables spice up the place. Don't hesitate to take a seat!

## + L'apéro

The ultimate French ritual which Parisians respect religiously. Starting about 6 pm, they unwind with friends before dinner, around a drink and some nibbles. If you're wondering what to order, try typical French aperitifs, like anise-flavored pastis, a glass of rosé wine, or un demi (beer from the tap). Kir or fortified wines like port or Pineau are also sweet possibilities. If you like bitter tastes and you're feeling adventurous, order a Suze, made from yellow gentian.

### La Favela Chic
DANCING

**18 Rue du Faubourg-du-Temple, 11th • M° République**
**www.favelachic.com • 01 40 21 38 14**
**Daily 9-2 am • Cover charge: €10**

La Favela Chic is nothing less than an institution. Located in a "hot" area near canal Saint-Martin, it positively sizzles inside, where the Brazilian ambience mixes it up with cheap but chic objects. There's a heady scent of caipirinha in the air. Huge community tables welcome you for dinner, but prefer drinks and partying to food... Friendly and laid-back, the Favela has been known to welcome dancing on the tables. It's a place to feel free and be wild.

### L'Orange Mécanique
DRINKS & MUSIC

**72 bis Rue Jean-Pierre-Timbaud, 11th**
**M° Parmentier**
**Monday-Saturday 8 pm-2 am**

The name of this bar says it all: it's ORANGE! Picture yourself in a boat on a river... Very seventies, and full of Vitamin C. It's a place for fun and good times (they probably never saw their namesake, A Clockwork Orange!), one of the cool addresses of the Rue Jean-Pierre-Timbaud. The program's full of events so don't be afraid you'll be bored: unplugged concerts, DJ mixes, themed parties, you name it!

### Le Café Charbon
DRINKS

**109 Rue Oberkampf, 11th • M° Saint Maur or Parmentier**
**Wednesday-Saturday 9-4 am; Sunday-Tuesday 9-2 am**

Café Charbon was one of the first outposts on Oberkampf, when it opened up to nightlife about ten years ago, and it remains one of the best. An all-oak interior with a zinc bar, it's the place to see and be seen by the neighborhood trendies heading for concerts at the Nouveau Casino next door.

My addresses around Canal Saint-Martin, République and La Villette

## Le 25° Est
DRINKS

**10 Place de la Bataille-de-Stalingrad, 19th • M° Jaurès or Stalingrad
01 42 09 66 74 • Daily 9-1 am**

Pronounce all the consonants, the way you've always wanted to say "est," even though your French teacher would never let you. This is "25 degrees East," a new spot right on the water which is poised for a position (thanks to coming renovation) as an "It" place in Paris. The food is supposed to be great but - can we be honest? - we always just sit there for hours soaking up the sun on the double-decker terrace, drinking rosé and dreaming that we're in Miami Beach.

## L'Alimentation Générale
DRINKS & LIVE MUSIC

**64 Rue Jean-Pierre-Timbaud, 11th • M° Parmentier
www.alimentation-generale.net • 01 43 55 42 50
Tuesday-Thursday 5:30 pm-2 am; Friday and Saturday 5:30 pm-4 am
No cover charge**

This former neighborhood grocery store on Rue Jean-Pierre-Timbaud is totally devoid of pretension, but that can be relaxing, and it keeps the prices down. Its ambition is to continue to serve the neighborhood, but with entertainment like a DJ mix jam every week instead of canned tuna. Check out the website for info.

## Lou Pascalou
DRINKS

**14 Rue des Panoyaux, 20th • M° Père-Lachaise
Daily 9-2 am, serving non-stop**

Lou Pascalou defines itself as an open-minded bar, so feel free to drop in for a late coffee, after a party or a show (certain other bars won't serve hot drinks after 10 pm). The live-and-let-live policy attracts artists, musicians, and writers, of course: how bohème could you be?!

## La Java
DRINKS & DANCING

**105 Rue du Faubourg-du-Temple, 10th • M° Belleville or Goncourt • 01 42 02 20 52
Monday-Saturday 7 pm-6 am • Cover charge: €5-25 (depending on the event)**

It's like a fairytale. This legendary club, where Edith Piaf got her start, slumbered, forgotten, for years, until Investor Charming came along and made it happening again. It now reigns as a funky, uninhibited dance and concert club, happily ever after, we hope! The neighborhood isn't fancy, but if you want to encounter the real Paris...

# Culture Mix

**H**ip and outdoorsy, the Canal and La Villette district is one of our personal favorites for culture: constantly surprising in its exhibition choices or special shows and events, it's also an opportunity to see contemporary architecture in the flesh, as it were...

## Le Plateau
CONTEMPORARY ART

**Place Hannah-Arendt • Rue des Alouettes at Rue Carducci, 19th**
**M° Jourdain or Buttes-Chaumont • www.fracidf-leplateau.com • 01 53 19 84 10**
**Wednesday-Friday 2-7 pm; Saturday-Sunday 12-8 pm • Admission: Free**

This 6,000-square-foot gallery is funded by the Ile-de-France region, one of 22 such administrations in continental France (historically heavy on bureaux), and shows works from their contemporary art collection, in addition to one or two temporary shows per year. It also occasionally holds concerts and performances: admission is then €4.

## Le Bataclan
LIVE MUSIC

**50 Boulevard Voltaire, 11th • M° Oberkampf**
**www.le-bataclan.com • 01 43 14 00 30 • Ticket prices varies**

This theater dates back to the wild years of the second half of the 19th century, and features playful pseudo-Oriental architecture. The colorful façade it sports today is simply a restoration of the original. It was named for one of composer Jacques Offenbach's light operas, which were ferociously popular at the time.. The programming has changed in the intervening years, but the Bataclan is still a successful hall. Today, diversity is a priority: the Bataclan raises its curtains for one-man shows, rock concerts, or private parties. It is one of those small theaters perfect for discovering indie artists.

## + Hunting for oldies but goodies

Select sharp vinyls! With all the DJ bars in this city, it's impossible for us not to tell you about the record stores, ideal for meeting the nightlife crowd. A great way to discover music new and old, and - why not? - dream of a turntable...
• **Ground Zero: 23 Rue Sainte-Marthe, 10th • M° Colonel-Fabien**
**01 40 03 83 08 • Monday-Saturday**
• **Crocodisc: 40 Rue des Écoles, 5th • M° Maubert-Mutualité**
**www.crocodisc.com • 01 43 54 33 22 •**
**Tuesday-Saturday. Closed for two weeks in the summer.**

## MK2 Quai de Seine & Quai de Loire

MOVIE THEATERS

**14 Quai de la Seine & 7 Quai de la Loire, 19th • M° Jaurès or Stalingrad**
**08 92 69 84 84**

Have you ever dreamed of going to see a movie by boat? Well, that's exactly what you might end up doing at this popular new Parisian spot. The MK2 theaters (an independent distribution company founded by director/producer Marin Karmitz, specializing in art-house films) are located on either side of the Canal de l'Ourcq, a branch of the Seine. Buy a ticket from the box office on one side, hop onto the little ferry, and cruise on across. To top the evening off, it's a pleasure to have an after-movie drink in one of the quiet cafés adjacent to the theaters. There's plenty of space for everyone to spread out, here in the canal district.

## Outdoor Screenings

This is a wonderful way to see a film. Every summer for five weeks (from mid-July to the end of August), a vast green lawn in La Villette Park welcomes cinema-lovers for special screenings. When night falls, the giant, drive-in-sized screen lights up with yet another grand illusion, casting the well-known spell on the audience. The program features recent films from all over the world, as well as classics. Equip yourself with a picnic, a sweater, and a blanket, and you're all set for a magical summer night in the city.

**Cinéma à La Villette**
**Parc de la Villette, Prairie du Triangle**
**M° Porte-de-Pantin**
**www.villette.com • 01 40 03 75 75**
**Check schedules and weather conditions**
**Tuesday to Sunday, July 15-August 31**
**Admission: Free • Deck chair rental: €6.50**

## Cinéma au Clair de Lune

The city of Paris offers free outdoor screenings of movies about Paris, during a three-week event in August which is not to be missed. Everyone is in the streets, watching movies about Paris together!
The event is organized by Le Forum des Images, a space dedicated to visual arts with an archive of still and motion-picture images of Paris. Movies are shown in a dozen different parks and squares. Be sure to check the website for programming and locations. In case of bad weather, screenings may be cancelled:

**www.clairdelune.forumdesimages.net • 01 44 76 63 00**

## Parc de la Villette
ARCHITECTURE & GARDENS

**211 Avenue Jean-Jaurès, 19th • M° Porte-de-Pantin**
**www.villette.com • 01 40 03 75 75**
**Information Center open daily 9:30 am-6:30 pm • Admission: Free**
**The park is open daily, but entrance is restricted between 1 and 6 am.**

The city's largest park (with the exception of the outlying Bois de Boulogne and Vincennes) sprawls blissfully over 130 acres, more than half of them green, and lies on either side of the Canal de l'Ourcq, where the stockyards and slaughterhouses once stood. Designed by Bernard Tschumi in 1982, its ultra-modern landscaping features long, clean lines and open spaces, as well as a number of smaller experimental "gardens" which are like the playgrounds of your dreams. It's an amazing place for a romp: people meet to play soccer or music, to do tai-chi, or simply to chat, away from the city traffic. A century of architecture is displayed on the La Villette grounds, from the 19th-century Grande Halle, to the grand-new Cité des Sciences et de

l'Industrie and Cité de la Musique. So far, there are also twenty-six Follies: red buildings with specific or silly functions, scattered around the lawns. In fact, the first building to catch your eye may be the Information Folly, a visitors' center on the main square outside the Métro station Porte-de-Pantin. It's small, compared to the Grande Halle, but it's vivid!

## ✚ Let's walk, bike, or cruise the Canals
**www.canalsaintmartin.fr**

Start where the canal comes aboveground, at the Rue du Faubourg-du-Temple. It's better to be on the left side (the Quai de Valmy) as you come up to the Place Stalingrad, so that you can connect to the Quai de la Loire, along the Bassin de la Villette (canals change names almost as often as streets).

By foot or bicycle, it's a charming promenade, an opportunity to stop at small cafés or improvise picnics. The lazy rhythm of the lock near Rue Beaurepaire is hypnotic: irresistibly relaxing.

The two-and-a-half-hour canal cruise takes you through the tunnel starting at Bastille, out into the open at Rue du Faubourg-du-Temple, and up to La Villette, climbing the series of locks as the hill rises. www.canauxrama.com - €15 per person

## Cité de la Musique
CONCERTS & EXHIBITIONS

**221 Avenue Jean-Jaurès, 19th • M° Porte-de-Pantin**
**www.cite-musique.fr • 01 44 84 44 84 • Admission: €7**
**Tuesday-Saturday 12 pm-6 pm; Sundays 10 am-6 pm. Closed January 1st, May**
**1st, August 15th, and December 25th**

The 11-building complex known as La Cité de la Musique is dedicated to studying, performing, sharing, and discovering music through the ages. Much of the emphasis is on Western music, although the institution does offer an ongoing gamelan workshop. Visitors can enjoy concerts performed by students at the national conservatory in addition to those of well-known musicians. Over 900 instruments are on display in the museum, a panoramic illustration of the history of music, and students sometimes demonstrate them for visitors. Christian de Portzamparc's architecture embraces the theme: the buildings are as dynamic and elegant as a symphony.

## Le 104
CONTEMPORARY ART

**104 Rue d'Aubervilliers, 19th • M° Stalingrad or Crimée**
**www.104.fr • 01 40 05 51 71 • Admission: Free**

Le 104 is the new contemporary art platform of the City of Paris. It houses galleries, auditoriums, artists' residences, and rehearsal space, not to mention a bookstore, a café, and a restaurant, in more than 260,000 square feet. This huge space used to be the municipal mortuary. Nowadays, definitely the place to be!

## Le Cabaret Sauvage
LIVE MUSIC

**Parc de la Villette 211 Avenue Jean-Jaurès, 19th • M° Porte-de-Pantin**
**www.cabaretsauvage.com • 01 42 09 01 09 • Check website for program**
**Snacks: €4-12 • Admission: €12-20**

Le Cabaret Sauvage is a vibrant multicultural crossroads, a circus big top with a large wooden dance floor, hosting a diversity of performances and events,

a place for urban nomads and gypsies where you can eat, drink, laugh, and dance. If you're lucky, you may enjoy a giant barbecue in the summer: check the website before going!

# Shopping Bobo

## American Apparel
FASHION (WOMEN/MEN/KIDS)

**10 Rue Beaurepaire, 10th • M° République**
**Monday-Saturday 10:30 am-7:30 pm**

If you adore the T-shirt attitude, come worship at the temple. This downtown Los Angeles brand has taken over Paris! Every fashion addict has at least one thing from American Apparel: the choice of styles and colors remains one of the chain's big plusses. Those casual hoodies are not only useful, they're trendy! American Apparel makes fashion accessible to women, men, kids and... dogs.
*T-shirt (from €22)*

## Liza Korn
FASHION (WOMEN/KIDS)

**19 Rue Beaurepaire, 10th • M° République**
**Monday-Saturday 10:30 am-7:30 pm**

Liza Korn has made a name for herself as THE Canal Saint-Martin designer: her studio is in the shop! Once you've admired the romantic dresses in sweet colors, check out the accessories: the purse necklace, vintage bags and trendy second-hand boots. You may find treasures for your kids... Try it out: you'll be welcomed with a smile.
*Purse necklace (€42) / Vintage bag (around €39)*

## Renhsen
FASHION (MEN/WOMEN)

**22 Rue Beaurepaire, 10th • M° République**
**01 48 04 01 01**
**Daily 9 am-7:30 pm (Sunday until 2 pm)**

An excellent spot for jeans, Renhsen has a great selection of brands as well as original creations. Sound, frank advice will guide you straight to the perfect jean cut for your figure. It's a heavy subject for us fashion victims. Never underestimate the power of pants.
*Jeans (from €150)*

## Coin Canal
FURNITURE & OBJECTS

**1 Rue de Marseille, 10th • M° Goncourt**
**01 42 38 00 30**
**Monday-Saturday 10 am-7 pm**

A cute furniture store right where Rue de Marseille meets Quai de Valmy, it's one of the best places to go for those pristine Scandinavian-style designs from the 50s and 60s. Prices are quite affordable, and you may find small items that will fit in your suitcase: candleholders, vases, or ashtrays, candy dishes. Even if you're simply browsing, it's an excellent school of style.
*Vase (around €12) / Desk (€1200)*

## Loulou Les Ames Arts
OBJECTS

**104 Quai de Jemmapes, 10th • M° Goncourt**
**06 11 42 35 98**
**Wednesday-Sunday 2-7 pm**

This shop is like a French grandmother's attic: crammed with everyday things from the first half of the 20th century which are rapidly becoming collectable. An ideal place to find little gifts with the French je ne sais quoi. Beware, the shop opens only after lunch.
*Glasses (€12) / Lamp (€200)*

## Médecine Douce
JEWELRY

**10 Rue de Marseille, 10th • M° Jacques-Bonsergent**
**01 48 03 57 28**

Médecine Douce may be a small shop, but it's a big problem for a Parisienne... Every piece of jewelry is amazing, and it breaks your heart to have to choose. Feathers, fetishes, primitive inspirations, and shamanistic talisman pendants gave the brand its name: properly tricked out as a medicine woman, you can heal all ills.
*Necklace (from €50)*

My addresses around Canal Saint-Martin, République and La Villette

# 8.

# Belleville
## and
# Buttes-Chaumont

Welcome to the east side! You're not in "postcard Paris" anymore: you've left the posh part of town behind. This part of Paris has plenty of public housing, inhabited by working-class people and immigrants, although the bobos are now beginning to take root. Visit Jim Morrison's tomb, browse flea markets, discover the city's most creative nightlife and, of course, the essential Parc des Buttes Chaumont. Paris will never be the same to you!

# Parisians'
## Secret
# Eateries

## Le Baratin

FRENCH ♦♦

**3 Rue Jouye-Rouve, 20th • M° Belleville**
**01 43 49 39 70**
**Tuesday-Friday 12-2:30 pm and 8-11 pm, Saturday 8-11 pm**

Standing on a West Village sidewalk, a chef in New York once told me, with utter conviction, "The best restaurant in Paris is Le Baratin"... What Le Baratin serves up is the opposite of its name, which means ballyhoo. Chef Raquel Caréla changes the menu daily, offering organic seasonal products, where originality meets tradition, and a great wine list. Atop Belleville, this restaurant is said to be a favorite with Paris's top chefs. Be sure to make reservations, because this small, beautiful pearl of a restaurant is in great demand.

## Le Faitout

FRENCH ♦

**23 Avenue Simon-Bolivar, 19th • M° Bolivar**
**01 64 08 01 29**
**Daily for lunch and dinner.**

A short walk from the Buttes Chaumont park, this restaurant has the camp charm of the east side of the capital: an old, high-ceilinged neighborhood bar, made ironic with a few post-modern touches. Nevertheless, there is absolutely no rush in this place: it's a hangout, where you can read the paper or play cards with your friends while listening to Bob Marley... smooth. Salads, veggie lasagnas, amazing quiches of the day, fruit salads...all is fresh and cheap.

## La Mère Lachaise

FRENCH ♦

**78 Boulevard de Ménilmontant, 20th • M° Père-Lachaise**
**01 47 97 61 60**
**Daily 9 am-2 pm; Saturday and Sunday for brunch**

A simple address between the Père Lachaise cemetery and Ménilmontant, La Mère Lachaise is a typical French neo-bistro: a new team has taken over an old bar and respected its essence (huge bar, old fashioned tiles, bentwood tables and chairs), placing even greater emphasis on the retro angle by hanging classroom charts and industrial lamps. Experiment with the three-course meal: leeks vinaigrette, tarragon chicken, and crème brulée or lemon pie... Unpretentious and quick. The terrace on the boulevard is relaxingly vast...

## Pho Dông Huông
VIETNAMESE ◆

**14 Rue Louis-Bonnet, 11th • M° Belleville**
**01 43 57 42 81 • Daily (except Tuesday) 12-10:30 pm**

Head here for a restorative pho, or soup, on a rainy day. The food is fresh and the walls aren't sticky. Your fellow Parisians are in on the secret too, though, and the place is always busy! Those star-spangled Belleville nights often begin here.

## The Night Time is the Right Time

Sociologically diverse, casual, young, and carefree crowds dance the nights away in Belleville, where the musical offer is varied. Low rents make it possible to cater to niche markets like rockers or country-music lovers, as well as the electro funk tectonic masses. Quintessentially Parisian and our favorite night spot.

## Studio de l'Ermitage
DRINKS & LIVE MUSIC

**8 Rue de l'Ermitage, 20th • Jourdain or Ménilmontant**
**www.studio-ermitage.com • 01 44 62 02 86**
**Cover charge: around €10**

A blessing on whoever subsidizes this large, no-frills venue where artists from a variety of genres perform. Be sure to check the schedule: there may be salsa, world music, saxophone bands... It's quite an enjoyable place to appreciate a show, with plenty of tables and a good view of the stage from the balcony. At their monthly dances, all ages and styles mix, and there's romance in the air...

## Les Folies
DRINKS

**8 Rue de Belleville, 19th • M° Belleville • Daily 7-2 am**

Les Folies, which was a cabaret in its youth, is enjoying a new life as a local bar, thronged at the cocktail hour (a prime moment in the typical Parisian's day!). If you're lucky, you'll be one of the happy few with a table on the terrace. Indoors, you can dig the typical Parisian touches like a long zinc counter and friendly bartender... The place belongs to Belleville and its inhabitants. Les Folies is no longer as wild as its name, but it absolutely screams for red wine!

# La Bellevilloise
DANCING

**19-21 Rue Boyer, 20th • M° Belleville**
**www.labelleviloise.com • 01 46 36 07 07**
**Wednesday-Friday 5:30 pm-2 am; Saturday-Sunday 11 am-2 pm**
**Friday and Saturday, DJ or live electro, 10 pm-6 am**
**Cover charge: €12; drinks: €5-9**

The place to go if you want to blow off some steam dancing. La Bellevilloise has long provided a roof for rebels. You'll find three or four different atmospheres: a restaurant, a huge bar in a loft, a rooftop (too rare in our city), and a club in the basement. An embarrassment of cultural riches! La Bellevilloise

propounds a dedication to light and creation on its website, but there's no rhetoric on the dance floor when the DJs are spinning soul, funk, and the best of Michael Jackson.

# La Flèche d'Or
DANCING

**102 bis Rue de Bagnolet, 20th**
**M° Porte-de-Bagnolet**
**www.flechedor.fr • 01 44 64 01 02**
**Daily 8-2 am**
**Usually no cover charge**

True, it's located in the eastern hinterlands, hence its freedom. You may have ridden a dozen Métro stations to get here – most of the hotels nearby are SROs – but you can now share in the rugged excitement of audacious live music. Located in a former railway station, the place has kept its industrial shell and welcomes an easygoing, fun crowd. Nobody will sneer at your shoes. Paris's rising musical and artistic stars cut loose here. A must.

# La Féline
MUSIC

**6 Rue Victor-Letalle, 20th • M° Ménilmontant**
**www.myspace.com/lafelinebar**

Wanna boogie? This pocket bar draws French fans of the American 50s look and, increasingly, those who gawk at them. Watch an Elvis Presley movie before the band starts to play (check their MySpace for samples). Meanwhile, out of the corner of your eye, admire the perfectly sprayed, slick pompadours on both guys and dolls! Is this ironic, or what? Don't forget your red lipstick!

# Culture Mix

## Le Père-Lachaise
CEMETERY

**15 Boulevard de Ménilmontant, 11th • M° Père-Lachaise**
**www.pere-lachaise.com • 01 43 71 91 66**
**Daily 8 am-5 pm**

It may seem strange to take a walk in a cemetery, but try it! You'll learn a lot about Paris and its history as you journey through time in this necropolis. The celebrities buried here are always drawing fans who pay their respects. There are legends about certain graves (Allan Kardec and Victor Noir come to mind), and this is where the left-wing rebels of the 1871 Commune, the Fédérés, made their last stand. Themed tours and maps are available at the entrance. Rock icon Jim Morrison's grave is a gathering place for Americans, whereas visiting Poles bring roses to Chopin.

## Parc des Buttes-Chaumont
GARDEN

**19th • M° Botzaris or Pyrénées**

Take the best nap of your life during working hours at the peaceful Buttes-Chaumont, a typical 19th-century creation. Napoleon III's urban-planning wizard Baron Haussmann, busy changing the face of the rest of Paris, delegated the landscape design on the 75-acre plot to Jean-Charles Alphand, who broke with the tradition of long, straight perspectives which had been in favor since the 17th century and introduced the English idea of the "natural-looking garden," with artificial cliffs, grottos, and waterfalls. Maybe this is what promotes the persistent rumors that the Sibyl Belvedere has magical properties, and that the old gypsum quarries beneath the park are the setting for bizarre occult rituals. You're not superstitious or anything, are you?

## Around Rue de la Mouzaïa

CHARMING AREA

**19th • M° Danube or Botzaris**

Discover a little-known village just a short walk from the Parc des Buttes-Chaumont. It'll feel like you stepped into a time warp. Small houses with gardens line quiet, narrow streets, quainter than quaint could be.

## "La Vie en Rose": Let's go back to the sources!

A shrine to Edith Piaf in Ménilmontant houses memorabilia related to the singer in a small apartment which is the property of an admirer so fervent he has written two biographies of her. The collection includes the little black dress and other evening gowns and day wear which once belonged to the artist, as well as posters, letters, sculptures, and photographs.

**Musée Édith Piaf:**
**5 Rue Crespin-du-Gast**
**Afternoons, by appointment only:**
**01 43 55 52 72**
**M° Ménilmontant**
**The tour is free, but please leave**
**a donation.**

After slumbering for decades, these southeastern borderlands are now thriving, linked to central Paris by the new, automated Métro line 14 (the one that no transit strike can shut down!). Catch a classic-masterpiece flick at the Cinémathèque at Bercy, then stroll through the gardens and across the Seine to an exhibit at the huge Bibliothèque Nationale. As you head westward to the Butte aux Cailles, a charming village behind the Place d'Italie, tarry a moment in Paris's unique Chinatown, along the Avenues d'Ivry and Choisy, stretching to Boulevard Masséna. You'll think you've been transported to another city, amid the plaster pagodas, Buddhist temples, and 70s skyscrapers and shopping centers. Specialty supermarkets like Tang Frères offer bargains on candied ginger, mangoes, almond cookies,

# 9.
# The New Paris:
## Around the
## Bibliothèque
### François-Mitterrand
## and the Parc de Bercy

and other Asian delights. Well worth a visit! Naturally, the streets are lined with cheap Chinese restaurants offering a thousand types of temptation.

Until the 1950s, barges loaded with barrels of wine used to travel up the Seine to the warehouses here, serving Paris's thirsty gullets. Disused for decades, the vast property now hosts two spectacular monoliths, the Ministry of Finances and the grass-sided POPB stadium. To the east, there's a 35-acre park (actually an ensemble of three gardens) to romp in, the Cinémathèque's spacious new digs, a shopping mall, and a museum of amusement-park attractions, open only by appointment, occasionally chartered by corporate clients...

# Parisians' Secret Eateries

## Chai 33
WORLD ◆◆

**33 Cour Saint-Émilion, 12th • M° Cour-Saint-Émilion**
**www.chai33.com • 01 53 44 01 01**
**Daily 9 am-11:30 pm; in addition to the breakfast, lunch, and dinner menus,**
**snacks are available at any time**

Located in an old wine warehouse on the Cour Saint-Emilion, this young, hip restaurant plays the wine card in an original way. A wine steward accompanies you into the cellar and helps you choose the perfect nectar to complement your meal. The food is simple: roasted lamb chops and mashed potatoes or chicken breasts on vegetables, but paired with the right wine, it's a ticket to ecstasy. After the meal, float through the romantic Bercy garden or do some shopping at Bercy Village. Animal-lovers, beware of the pet shop! It won't be easy to fly home with that cocker spaniel puppy. Are you staying in Paris?

## ✚ Let's be snobs!

In the mood for dim sum dumplings? Dare to dig into a durian? Go to the source: Chinatown's vast Asian supermarket **Tang Frères**.

**Tang Frères: 48 Avenue d'Ivry, 13th • M° Olympiades**
**01 45 85 19 85 • Tuesday-Sunday 9 am-7:30 pm**

## Les Cailloux
ITALIAN ♦♦

**58 Rue des Cinq-Diamants, 13th • M° Corvisart**
**01 45 80 15 08**
**Tuesday-Saturday for lunch and dinner**

A trattoria atop the Butte aux Cailles, a cobblestone district Parisians have been keeping to themselves. Prices are almost as steep as the Butte, but you will be discovering Italian wines and neo-Italian cuisine (linguini with crabmeat, apple, and pear sauce; bruschetta with vegetables). Since it already attracts crowds of locals, please keep this address secret, and phone for reservations before setting out.

## Chez Paul
FRENCH ♦♦

**22 Rue de la Butte-aux-Cailles, 13th**
**M° Corvisart or Place-d'Italie**
**01 45 89 22 11**
**Monday-Sunday 12-2 pm and 7 pm-12 am**

Another temple of traditional Lyonnais cuisine, heavy on meats. If you refer to those as "animal fats," this is not the place for you. Chez Paul plays expert riffs on the classics, the pâtés, the roast suckling pig with sage, the grilled sea bass... Food that sticks to your ribs! Life is sweet on the shady restaurant terrace, and that's always excellent for your digestion.

## Café Fusion
FRENCH FUSION ♦♦

**12 Rue de la Butte-aux-Cailles, 13th • M° Corvisart • 01 45 80 12 02**
**Tuesday-Saturday 12-3 pm and 7-11:30 pm**

Fusion cuisine, the latest touchstone of fashionable restaurants, is not everyone's cup of tea. However, one meal at Café Fusion will silence the critics. They'll be wooed by colombo-coconut chicken crumble, the duck with candy-coated roses, or pork, ginger, and lemon-grass stir-fry, and if they aren't, that perennial classic, the hamburger, is still on the menu. The location's other assets include an especially pleasant dining room and a magnificent terrace, a welcome roost for the weary. Lunchtime is quiet, but the energy goes up a notch at night. In any case, it's 100% cheerful.

## Chez Gladines
SOUTHWEST FRENCH ◆

**30 Rue des Cinq-Diamants, 13th • M° Corvisart • 01 45 80 70 10**
**Monday-Saturday 12-3 pm and 7 pm-12 am; Sunday 12-4 pm**
**Gigantic salads:  5-9; potatoes:  5-7; cold cuts and cheeses:  4-8.50; entrées:  7-11**

A bargain Basque bistro which has invested in food rather than interior design, making a specialty of assuaging the most ferocious appetites with huge salads. The potato-chips-and-Basque-delicatessen platter also has its fans. Laughter and wine flow freely. Your best bet is to stay away from the hot entrées.

## Lao Douang Chan
LAOTIAN ◆

**161 Avenue de Choisy, 13th • M° Tolbiac • 01 44 24 80 80**
**Daily (except Tuesday) 12:30-2:30 pm and 7:30-10:30 pm**

My Dubai friends head straight for this tiny restaurant as soon as they get off the plane! Even though it looks identical to the dozen other Laotian restaurants on the boulevard, the food is so fabulous it must be tasted to be believed. Try the chicken and banana flower salad, the spicy beef salad, and, once you've come back to your senses, send us an e-mail...

**+** Head straight to nirvana: make an offering to the **Parisian Buddhist Temple**.
**Centre Teochew de Méditation Bouddhique:**
**44 Avenue d'Ivry (On the upper level**
**of the Olympiades mall, follow the hallway to**
**your right as you leave the shopping center)**
**M° Porte-d'Ivry**
**01 45 82 06 01 • Daily 9 am-12 pm and 2-6 pm**

## Chinatown Olympiades
CHINESE ◆◆

**44 Avenue d'Ivry, 13th • M° Porte-d'Ivry or Olympiades**
**www.chinatownolympiades.com • 01 45 84 72 21**
**Daily 11:45 am-2:45 pm and 6:45 pm-1 am**

The Paris culinary experience has been enriched by the Chinese diaspora, with 35,000 immigrants in this area alone. The community has now been here for two generations, but the ancestral recipes are being preserved. Give the Chinatown Olympiades a whirl. This large eating house is 200% Chinese! A special room proposes karaoké and dancing all day long. Don't forget your passport!

# The Night Time is the Right Time

The area has grown more and more popular for its nightlife, since several clubs are now fixtures in the barges, right on the water, where there aren't many neighbors to disturb. Slightly upmarket and preppy, compared to Belleville, but still local and fun.

## Le Djoon
DANCING

**22-24 Boulevard Vincent-Auriol, 13th • M° Quai-de-la-Gare**
**www.djoon.fr • 01 45 70 83 49**
**Thursday-Saturday starting at 12 am; Sunday starting at 6 pm**

This is a taste of New York in Paris: a loft serving dinner and drinks, and an irresistible dance floor, where you can get down! The soulful groove is surely a part of the place, and the funky urban crowd will make you feel at ease: high heels meet fashionable sneakers. Unpretentious and truly chic, it embodies the dynamism of a neighborhood on the rise. An ideal place to spend hours with your friends and even meet new ones – why not?

Don't waste your time waiting in line at the taxi station, if the Métro stops running before the party's over... Hop on a **Vélib** and pedal home singing (see p. 143)

## Le Batofar
DANCING

**In front of 11 Quai François-Mauriac, 13th**
**M° Quai-de-la-Gare or Bibliothèque-François-Mitterrand**
**www.batofar.org • 01 53 60 17 30**
**Daily • Cover charge: €0-25 (depending on the event)**

For a decade now, le Batofar has been attracting Parisians to these 13th-arrondissement banks of the Seine on the city's eastern limits. This red lighthouse-boat rocks with electronic parties, but offers a great variety of other kinds of music (funk, rock, hip-hop, reggae soundsystems, etc.). In this fantastic place, 3,000 square feet of dance floor and three differents bars welcome you. Not only that, when the sun comes out, the party begins on the dock. With the new national library towering overhead, it just doesn't feel like Paris anymore. What a treat!

# La Dame de Canton
DRINKS & LIVE MUSIC

**Port de la Gare, 13th • M° Quai-de-la-Gare or**
**Bibliothèque-François-Mitterrand**
**Tuesday-Thursday 7 pm-2 am; Friday-Saturday**
**7 pm till dawn; Sunday 12:30 pm-12 am**
**See website for events**
**www.damedecanton.com • 01 53 61 08 49**
**Cover charge: variable • Dinner €24-30**

The Chinese junk moored on the Quai de la Gare is once again known as La Dame de Canton, her maiden name, after a spell as La Guinguette Pirate. Offering an intimate setting for world music (heavy on the Balkans) as well as house mixes, by day it is popular as a sunny waterfront venue where you can grab a snack. Relax and party as the Seine flows by...

Treat yourself to a **Chinese massage**, quite unsophisticated but efficient and really cheap. One of the best offers in Paris!
**Dong Fang Relaxation:**
**12 Rue Caillaux, 13th • 01 44 23 91 70**
**M° Maison-Blanche**
**Daily 12-10 pm**

# La Folie en Tête
DRINKS

**33 Rue de la Butte-aux-Cailles, 13th • M° Corvisart • 01 45 80 65 99**
**Monday-Saturday 6 pm-2 am**

If you find your way to the Butte aux Cailles (and you should), don't miss this authentic little bar. In the heart of the village, La Folie en Tête is proof that good things come in small packages. Live music and discussion are always on tap. The locals are friendly, so don't be shy.

My addresses around the Bibliothèque François-Mitterrand and the Parc de Bercy

This new Paris district has grown up a lot in fifteen years, and is now a sassy teenager. The neighborhoods bordering the waterfront used to be a no-man's-land with a whiff of danger about them, but ambitious architectural achievements and well-planned transportation and housing have definitively dispelled that aura. Who said Paris was turning into a museum city?!

## Cinémathèque Française
EXHIBITIONS & FILMS

**51 Rue de Bercy, 12th • M° Bercy**
**www.cinematheque.fr • 01 71 19 33 33 • Admission: Films, €6; exhibits, €5**
**Exhibits: Monday-Saturday 12 pm-7 pm; Thursday 12-10 pm;**
**Sunday 10 am-8 pm.**
**Screenings: Daily (except Tuesday)**

Likening it to "a ballerina lifting her tutu," architect Frank Gehry designed the vast building as an American cultural center, but funding for this type of initiative had dried up during the Reagan era, and for ten years, the space was vacant. Finally, in 2005, the French national film archive, the Cinémathèque, opened five auditoriums here, on the edge of the contemporary Parc de Bercy. They also stage exciting temporary exhibits providing insight into every aspect of the seventh art: directing, costumes, sets, history... Screenings revolve around various themes, honoring giants from all times and countries or premiering new releases. Paris can be proud of this resource, where aspiring filmmakers can devour the classics the way François Truffaut and Jean-Luc Godard did, at the old Palais de Chaillot. Maybe it'll launch a new New Wave!

## Passerelle Simone de Beauvoir
ARCHITECTURE

**From Quai François-Mauriac (in front of the BNF) to Quai de Bercy**
**and Parc de Bercy, 12th • M° Quai-de-la-Gare**

Lovers of modern architecture will say the capital city's newest bridge, its thirty-seventh, is its most poetic. Open to pedestrian traffic alone, it effortlessly sweeps the explorer across the Seine, from the 12th to the 13th arrondissement, depositing him or her on either an upper or a lower level. The 900-foot promenade, named for the author and philosopher who practically invented French feminism, provides a panorama of the less traditional, but still beautiful, parts of the city. Quite fitting.

# Bibliothèque François-Mitterrand (BNF)
FRANCE'S NATIONAL LIBRARY

**Quai François-Mauriac, 13th • M° Bibliothèque-François-Mitterrand**
**www.bnf.fr • 01 53 79 59 59 • Admission: Free**
**Tuesday-Saturday 10 am-7 pm; Sunday 1 pm-7 pm**
**Closed January 1st, May 1st, and December 25th**

Every French president has an "edifice complex," and this is how François Mitterrand, who served from 1981 to 1995, gratified his. It opens the door to a whole new neighborhood in the capital, the 13th arrondissement Paris Rive Gauche. The controversial design, by architect Dominique Perrault, has been said to resemble four books standing on their spines. The national library houses every single manuscript and document ever printed in France.

Wandering through the monumental structure is an experience in itself. Inside, you can browse special photography exhibits (for the national library also archives photographs, of course) and access books and periodicals, from the popular to the scholarly. The lower floors are off limits to all except researchers and students: a garden gives a natural touch for inspiration and meditation.

# Cité de la Mode et du Design
ARCHITECTURE

**Les Docks de Paris: Quai de la Gare, 13th • M° Quai-de-la-Gare**

La Cité de la Mode et du Design is a brand new architectural creation impatient to open. Its first tenant is slated to be the IFM, the Paris Fashion Institute (www.ifm-paris.com), an institution which provides advanced training in fashion design. Perfect for this spaceship on the edge of the Seine River. Architects Jakob & MacFarlane have imagined the "blob" as a contemporary venue for Parisians with a promenade, restaurants, and shops. A spectacular New Paris sight!

# Butte-aux-Cailles one-upmanship

Compared to the lofty heights of Montmartre and Belleville (almost 390 feet), the Butte-aux-Cailles seems like a puny hill, only 180 feet above sea level. The Cailles were not quails but a family of farmers or millers who gave their name to this piece of real estate back in the 16th century. Until about 1850, there were practically no buildings on the Butte, aside from a few rural farm sheds, rickety wooden shacks standing at the entrances to the many clay and stone quarry pits here.

Once part of Gentilly, the Butte was annexed to Paris in 1860. Laundresses, ragpickers, and shoe-industry workers moved in. Living from day to day and from hand to mouth, they slowly built modest dwellings, atop the quarry pits, which were not always well filled. It was not until after 1910, when the Bièvre River was covered, that the semi-rural enclave on the hill became fully urban.

In recent years, the Butte has become fashionable. Its bars and restaurants are flourishing, and visitors crowd in to discover the relaxed, friendly village atmosphere, with its staunch anarchist-trade-union roots. The neighborhood's working-class dwellings, with their postage-stamp-sized gardens, have miraculously survived to become highly coveted properties for the newly affluent...

**La Petite Alsace: 10 Rue Daviel, 13th**
**Villa Daviel: 7 Rue Daviel, 13th**
**Cité Fleurie: 65 Boulevard Arago, 13th**
**All three are close to M° Glacière**

I Love Paris

Cole Porter

I love Paris in the springtime,
I love Paris in the fall,
I love Paris in the winter when it drizzles,
I love Paris in the summer when it sizzles,

I love Paris every moment,
Every moment of the year.
I love Paris, why oh why do I love Paris?
Because my love is near.

# Getting
# some sleep

The first time you travelled to Paris, you may have ended up in a soulless chain hotel, in a room that could have been in any city. This time, we think you deserve to stay in the kind of hotel that Parisians would recommend to their friends, and that some of them have actually tried themselves. The suggestions below include both modern and old-fashioned hotels, but all have that typical Paris touch, located in picturesque, pleasant neighborhoods. Good prices and service are also on the menu, but if you're on a budget, make sure you book early! (See p. 6 for the map).

| | |
|---|---|
| € | 60 to 90 euros per room, per night |
| €€ | 100 to 200 euros per room, per night |
| €€€ | 200 euros and more per room, per night |

## Au Relais Saint-Honoré ***
OPÉRA & PALAIS-ROYAL

**308 Rue Saint-Honoré, 1st • M° Louvre-Rivoli**
**sainthonore.free.fr • 01 42 96 06 06**

The fulfillment of your ultimate Parisian fantasy... The entrance to the Louvre is right around the corner, and it's only a five-minute walk to the Opera, and Tuileries Gardens. Your temporary home will be a 17th-century building in the heart of this city's shopping and cultural scene. After the day's bustle has subsided, the Rue Saint-Honoré is quiet and peaceful at night, allowing you to enjoy your beauty sleep. It's exhausting, being a Parisian! €€

## Le Relais du Louvre ***
OPÉRA & PALAIS-ROYAL

**19 Rue des Prêtres-Saint-Germain-l'Auxerrois, 1st • M° Louvre-Rivoli**
**www.relaisdulouvre.com • 01 40 41 96 42**

Mona Lisa and the Venus de Milo will be watching over your sleep in this comfortable, quiet hotel facing the Louvre. It, too, is convenient to a number of attractions. Allow us to recommend a peek inside the beautiful white Gothic church adjacent to the hotel, built for royal worship. Le Fumoir bar and restaurant is also nearby, and perfect for a nightcap.. A total experience. €€

## Little Palace Hotel ***
BASTILLE, MARAIS & CHÂTELET

**4 Rue Salomon-de-Caus, 3rd • M° Réaumur-Sébastopol**
**www.littlepalacehotel.com • 01 42 72 08 15**

This elegant, modern hotel hidden inside a turn-of-the-century apartment building complete with marble columns and decorative carved stone is well-located on the edge of a small park, in the heart of the city, convenient to the Centre Pompidou and the Marais area. Its 53 rooms and 4 suites have just been redecorated, so it's brand new. Peace, quiet, privacy, and refinement can be yours at a reasonable price. €€

## Le Petit Moulin ***
BASTILLE, MARAIS & CHÂTELET

**29/31 Rue de Poitou, 3rd • M° Saint-Sébastien-Froissart**
**www.paris-hotel-petitmoulin.com • 01 42 74 10 10**

The jewel of the Upper Marais, Le Petit Moulin is a boutique hotel, a hidden place symbolizing the new Parisian chic. Decorated by fashion designer Christian Lacroix, each room is a work of art, sparkling with genius and loopy with his signature rococo style. You'll feel like nesting here for the rest of your life, just going out for baguettes and romantic dinners, and maybe some funky shopping Rue Vieille-du-Temple... Your new life is all set up! €€€

## Hôtel du Vieux Marais **
BASTILLE, MARAIS & CHÂTELET

**8 Rue du Plâtre, 4th • M° Rambuteau**
**www.vieuxmarais.com • 01 42 78 47 22**

An all-white-and-pinewood hotel in the Marais. Charm is not its forte, unless you're an unshakeable modernist, but it provides you with a pied-à-terre in one of the city's most exciting neighborhoods, convenient to everything! The simplicity of the place is enhanced by the friendly team: what more do you need?! €€

The **boutique-hotel concept** has arrived in Paris and, of course, it's a hit! Designers like Philippe Starck and artists like Sophie Calle, André, and Jérôme Mesnager have had a field day, commissioned to create rooms that conjure up dreams and fantasies.... For a complete guide to the city's most stylish accommodations:
*Hôtels chic et intimes* by Lionel Paillès, in French and English, Editions Parigramme

## La MIJE
BASTILLE, MARAIS & CHÂTELET

**6 Rue de Fourcy, 4th** • M° Saint-Paul or Pont-Marie
**11 Rue du Fauconnier, 4th** • **M° Saint-Paul or Pont-Marie**
**12 Rue des Barres, 4th** • **M° Saint-Paul or Pont-Marie**
**www.mije.com • 01 42 74 23 45**

You'd call it a bargain; Parisians would admit it was a "bon plan": simple but affordable accommodation for young people located in a cluster of three 17th-century mansions, complete with courtyards and exposed beams, right in the Marais. The rates are unbeatable, but the reservation policy is strict: you can't book the room more than 45 days in advance, except for August stays, when you can make reservations the previous February (six months ahead of time) - and you'll probably need to! The MIJE also provides a cafeteria dinner (€10.50) and can help plan your visit to Paris or excursions elsewhere in France. **€**

## ✚ Let's be snobs!

The charm of **Studio 22** is ineffable, but one can try to describe it. The Marais location is undoubtedly a contributing factor. Next, it opens onto a communal courtyard that reminds us of a Victor Hugo novel. Its subtle black-and-white interiors, combining a symphony of notes, are fit to fulfill the dreams of any guest. But the Studio 22 concept is the main attraction: the hostesses, artists themselves, offer their guests the various art services they themselves wish they had when they are traveling: advice on temporary shows, gallery openings, and even introductions to artists. Our future will surely need places like this, far removed from official art, institutions, yet suffused with beauty, where pleasure is not only a goal in itself but also a means to an end. Massages for exhausted art-lovers available on request. **€€**

**www.lestudio22.com • 06 60 13 98 20**

## Hôtel Duo ★★★
BASTILLE, MARAIS & CHÂTELET

**11 Rue du Temple, 4th** • M° Hôtel-de-Ville
**www.duo-paris.com • 01 42 72 72 22**

A style that is simultaneously contemporary and welcoming, with an aura of gourmet flavors - vanilla, coffee and chocolate. Armchairs upholstered in hound's-tooth check or aniseed green, lampshades sporting botanical filigrees; a virtual fireplace with a video display, 70s-style furniture...A breath of fresh air! **€€**

### Hôtel Saint-Louis ★★★

BASTILLE, MARAIS & CHÂTELET

**75 Rue Saint-Louis-en-l'Île, 4th • M° Pont-Marie**
**01 46 34 04 80**
**www.hotelsaintlouis.com • free WIFI access**

On timeless Île Saint-Louis, this hotel is convenient to the restaurants and shops on the island's main street, where automobile traffic is rare. You'll have to cross the bridge to take the Métro, but that's the price you pay for your splendid isolation. The hectic streets, though only a five-minute walk away, are merely a distant memory in this quiet backwater in central Paris. This family-owned hotel, offering plain, simple rooms – always restful – gives you a warm welcome, into the bargain. €€

### Hôtel des Grandes Écoles ★★★

QUARTIER LATIN

**75 Rue du Cardinal-Lemoine, 5th • M° Cardinal-Lemoine or Place-Monge**
**01 43 26 79 23**

This delightful hotel is located in a pink 19th-century townhouse atop a rise, in the middle of a garden, where you can easily imagine yourself relaxing after a long day of trudging the streets. You wouldn't be surprised to

encounter a Belle Epoque lady having tea there. The interiors are rather corny: get ready for macramé and printed toile-de-Jouy wallpaper. Just what a French grandmother would love. But don't worry, it's clean and simple. There's no TV, but with Paris out there, who needs it? Slightly kitsch, but surely romantic. Try it! €€

### Hôtel Pas-de-Calais ★★★

SAINT-GERMAIN-DES-PRÉS

**59 Rue des Saints-Pères, 6th • M° Sèvres-Babylone**
**www.hotelpasdecalais.com • 01 45 48 78 74**
**Free internet access in the lobby.**

The Rue des Saints-Pères is the shopping addicts' downfall, where temptations are manifold! and now we've gone and found a lovers' nest in a district where you're liable to fry your Visa card at the galleries and boutiques. Le Pas-de-Calais is a family hotel, where the owner has decorated every room differently. It all remains tasteful and Parisian (synonymous, aren't they?), with simple lines and a cosy wooden staircase. This calm haven of a hotel is even staffed by warm, friendly people. Be sure to have a drink in the glass-ceilinged lobby, and feel free to admire the amazing green wall, pride of the hotel... €€

### L'Atelier des Beaux-Arts ***
SAINT-GERMAIN-DES-PRÉS

**8 Rue de la Grande-Chaumière, 6th** • M° Vavin
**www.latelierdesbeauxarts.com** • 01 40 47 78 67

Didn't you murmur something about wanting to live the life of a real Parisian? Here is the opportunity to have a place you can call your own. This loft, located in one of the finest neighborhoods of the capital, can be all yours for two days or a week. It's beautifully designed for a cosy, independent stay. Needless to say, you must book well in advance. But the day will come when you can buy your cheese and wine and invite your new Parisian friends over! **€€**

## ➕ Sleep in a Parisian bed

Parisians are finally overcoming a strong cultural barrier and starting to open up to the prospect of sharing or exchanging their home with complete strangers. Couchsurfing is just around the corner! To exchange your home for a Parisian apartment,

**www.homelink.fr**
**www.craigslist.org**
**www.trocmaison.com**
**www.trocky.com**
**www.homeforexchange.com**

## ➕ To find a B&B in Paris

A few rooms for rent in a house... with a swimming pool! Artists' studios in need of paying guests while the regular tenants are in Berlin for a show! Charming old ladies supplementing their pensions by renting out the empty rooms in their vast apartments... Little by little, the idea of taking in boarders, fairly common in the countryside but rare in Paris, is catching on. Every offer is unique, but visitors are invariably grateful to obtain such high-quality hospitality at a low price (around €60 for a room for two) The deals on the websites below will make your heart beat faster!

**www.chambre-ville.com** • 01 44 06 96 71
**www.goodmorningparis.fr** 01 47 07 28 29
**www.bed-and-breakfast-in-paris.com**

## Hôtel Amour
PIGALLE

**8 Rue de Navarin, 9th • M° Pigalle**
**www.hotelamour.com • 01 48 78 31 80 (reservations only by phone)**

This is the small hotel creating the big buzz, in a quiet street south of Pigalle, with only 20 rooms. Not only that, all the rooms were decorated by prominent contemporary artists. The atmosphere is olé-olé, as the French say: the perfect place to make kids rather than bring them... Rooms are so ultra-modern that they relegate television and landlines to the dustbin of history, but provide an iPod base. The "no decoration" restaurant and bar puts the focus on people. Make sure to eat in the garden: it's a jewel... €€

**+ Let's be snobs!**

Organize a **private dinner party** at Hôtel Amour – just give them two months' notice:

**Hôtel Amour: Dining room (€200 ).**
**Dinner (€40 per guest). Bartender (€80 )**
**www.hotelamour.com • 01 48 78 31 80**

## Hôtel Lorette-Opéra ***
PIGALLE

**36 Rue Notre-Dame-de-Lorette, 9th • M° Notre-Dame-de-Lorette**
**www.loretteopera.com • 01 42 85 18 81**

A contemporary hotel, the Lorette is one of those new addresses that propose a chic, designer atmosphere and impeccable service for a good price... Just south of the Pigalle area and near the place Saint-George, it's ideally situated. You'll be walking distance to Montmartre, the department stores, and the Opera, and a Métro ride away from the funky east of Paris. Design meets cobblestones in the Hôtel Lorette, but the décor remains sober. A patio will let you enjoy a moment of calm before hitting the streets! €€€

## Hôtel du Nord **
CANAL SAINT-MARTIN

**47 Rue Albert-Thomas, 10th • M° République or Jacques-Bonsergent**
**www.hoteldunord-leparivelo.fr • 01 42 01 66 00**

The Hotel du Nord is a dream come true: it's exactly how you'd imagine comfortable accommodations in Paris, like staying in a family house filled with souvenirs, soft velvet upholstery, and quiet conversation. The location, along Canal Saint-Martin, is ideal for travelers who love to roam the streets, taking long walks and enjoying espresso in a neighborhood that is still Starbucks-free. A jewel! Free bikes available from the hotel. €

### Le Général ★★★
RÉPUBLIQUE

**5-7 Rue Rampon, 11th • M° Oberkampf**
**www.legeneralhotel.com • 01 47 00 41 57**

Newly decorated with a mix of young, fresh design in classical buildings, this hotel proposes excellent quality for a good price in the calm, neighborly streets on the east side of Paris. Services include a bar and gym. These boutique hotels offer so much solicitude and personal attention to their guests that the

comfort level approaches that of a luxury hotel, without the hype and extra expense. Special offers if you reserve on the website. **€€**

### Le Quartier hotel - République, Le Marais ★★
RÉPUBLIQUE

**39 Rue Jean-Pierre-Timbaud, 11th • M° Parmentier**
**www.quartier-hotel-republique-paris.federal-hotel.com • 01 48 06 64 97**

The little sister of Le General Hotel above Le Quartier République, Le Marais is cheaper but remains a quality place to stay. On quiet Rue Jean-Pierre Timbaud, a stone's thrown from the Canal Saint-Martin and Place de la République, this hotel is just over the boundary from the Marais, within convenient walking distance. It's an ideal location if you've already done the central-Paris circuit on your first visit to Paris and are ready to explore the hipster east side. The bedrooms are small but comfy, with funky details and little extras. After working out and having a sauna, refresh yourself with a fruit cocktail in the bright, colorful bar. **€**

### Le Standard Design Hôtel ★★★
BASTILLE

**29 Rue des Taillandiers, 11th • M° Voltaire or Bastille**
**www.standard-design-hotel-paris.com • 01 48 05 30 97**

Le Standard is a brand-new hotel near Rue de Charonne and Bastille, belonging to the new generation of boutique hotels where the emphasis is on design and modernity. If you prefer the old-fashioned look (we find it corny, ourselves), this is not the place for you. Nevertheless, the excellent accommodations and ideal location, convenient for dining and dancing, may make a convert out of you. On Friday and Saturday nights, fun-seeking Parisians know this area is the place to find it. **€€**

## Le Quartier hotel - Bastille **

BASTILLE

**9 Rue de Reuilly, 12th • M° Faidherbe-Chaligny**
**www.lequartierhotelbf.com • 01 43 70 04 04**

Slick and shiny, consummately contemporary: the interiors are a clean, fresh mixture of chrome, glass, plastic, and polyester. Simplicity is the handmaiden of modernism. No one will have to twist your arm to get you to have breakfast or a drink on the landscaped terrace which is one of the hotel's biggest selling points. The "Le Quartier" chain operates a number of hotels on the east side of Paris, around Place de la République and Bercy. Special offers are often available online. €€

**New address a bit farther east: Le Quartier - Bercy, Square** (€€)**
**33 Boulevard de Reuilly, 12th • M° Daumesnil or Dugommier**
**www.lequartierhotelbs.com • 01 44 87 09 09**

## Villa Toscane

INVALIDES

**36-38 Rue des Volontaires, 15th • M° Volontaires**
**www.hotelvillatoscane.fr • 01 43 06 82 92**

This seven-room hotel is totally boudoir, old-fashioned and overwrought, but in an inexplicably chic way... Your stay will definitely be romantic! It's one of the poshest hotels in the south of Paris. The 15th arrondissement is calm, with a bourgeois, family atmosphere that is quite comfortable to come home to, after you've traipsed through the Left Bank galleries and bookstores – unless you've been clothes-shopping again! Rooms are available at a good price on a monthly basis. €€

## Hôtel Eldorado **

BATIGNOLLES

**18 Rue des Dames, 17th • M° Place-de-Clichy**
**www.eldoradohotel.fr • 01 45 22 35 21**

Absolutely enchanting, and the best price-to-charm ratio of any hotel in the city. It has everything on the bohemian globetrotter's wishlist: a quiet garden, low prices, vintage furniture, a reading room, and one of the town's most sought-after garden restaurants next door. If you want minimalism or design, try another address! The Eldorado is a hotel with a soul, and like all incredible places, it's so popular it fills up fast, so be sure to book early. A haven of calm in the city, a short walk from both Montmartre and Les Batignolles, and you're linked to Belleville and Ménilmontant directly by Métro. Go for it! €

## Hôtel Caulaincourt Square *
MONTMARTRE

**2 square Caulaincourt, 18th • M° Lamarck-Caulaincourt**
**www.caulaincourt.com • 01 46 06 46 06**

On the other side of Montmartre, far from the roar of the tourist crowd, this is your typical budget hostel: you have to accept the idea of community to book a dorm room! But the location is ideal, under magnificent trees, just at the foot of one of those charming Montmartre stairs, on a street filled with good restaurants and cafés. **€**

## Ermitage Hôtel **
MONTMARTRE

**24, rue Lamarck, 18th**
**M° Lamarck-Caulaincourt**
**01 42 64 79 22 • www.ermitagesacrecoeur.fr**
**(reserve only by phone)**

This 12-room hotel perched on Montmartre hill is reminiscent of a boarding house. What we like about this hermitage is the Napoleon III architecture and its secret weapon: a heartrendingly beautiful view from a terrace overlooking Paris. It may be old-fashioned, but it's so unique it's irresistible. **€**

## Mama Shelter
BELLEVILLE

**109, rue de Bagnolet, 20th • 01 43 48 48 48**
**www.mamashelter.com**

Édith Piaf and Jim Morrison - both buried in Père-Lachaise Cemetery - might haunt this outlying neighborhood, which is part artists' lofts, part single-family dwellings, "the country in Paris." But there's more to life than mere nostalgia! And Mama Shelter was designed by Philippe Starck, determined to make this hotel just across the street from the Flèche d'Or nightclub a big, affectionate mother of a shelter where guests can meet artists from all over the world, in residence there. Note that the 172 rooms are equipped with iMacs and bedding worthy of a five-star hotel. Moreover, the restaurant is not bad at all. **€€**

# Tips
# for feeling at home in Paris

## How to get around?

We strongly advise against driving in Paris, for two very good reasons. First of all, Parisians are crazy drivers. Secondly, if you do manage to arrive safely at your destination, you might never find a place to park!

### The Métro and buses are what you need!

• Métros run until 1 am on weekdays and 2 am on weekends. After that, the Noctambus night buses take over, ferrying the nightowls home.

• If you want to enjoy a great view of Paris, cheap, ride the elevated Métro lines: 2 (Nation-Porte-Dauphine) is skyborne between Barbès and Jaurès; line 6 (Nation-Charles-de-Gaulle-Étoile), between Passy and Pasteur.

• Want a bus tour for the price of a Métro ticket? Take the 95 from Montmartre to Porte de Vanves. It passes Place de Clichy, Trinité, Opéra, Palais-Royal, Musée du Louvre, and the Musée d'Orsay, before rolling down posh Boulevard Saint-Germain, to Sèvres-Babylone and Vavin.

**Métro and bus (RATP): ticket (€1.50 ) • Weekly commuter pass (unlimited, but valid only Monday-Sunday) (€16.30) • Paris Visite tourist pass (€8.50 a day or €27.50 for 5 days) • Noctambus: 5 bus lines (12:30-5:30 am) • www.ratp.fr**

### Hep taxis!

Taxis can be pretty hard to find in Paris after le dernier Métro or at rush hour. Available taxis have a white light on their roof. When they are taken, the light turns orange. You can hail a cab in the street or wait at a taxi station, signaled by a blue sign. The fare starts at €2, and the minimum fare is €5. Few taxis accept credit cards, so be sure to carry some cash. If you're tempted to take a taxi to the airport due to excessive luggage or ungodly hours, make a reservation the night before.

**G7: 01 47 39 47 39 • www.taxis-g7.fr**
**Taxis Bleus: 01 49 36 24 24 • 08 25 16 24 24 • 08 91 70 10 10 • www.taxis-bleus.com**
**Alpha: 01 45 85 85 85 • www.alphataxis.fr**

## The new Parisian kick: Vélib

This self-service rental bicycles available 24 hours a day, 7 days a week, with stations located all around the city is a real hit. To rent one, all you need is a "smart" credit card with a microchip and your PIN code, to leave the €150 deposit on the bike. Just follow the instructions in English on the terminal. And harken to the voice of experience: look the bikes over carefully before you begin the process. Details to check: tires, chain, and, last but not least, the quick-release lever on the seat-adjustment bolt, which sometimes falls victim to metal fatigue. Of course, if you get a bum bike, you can always trade it in, but you're on your way somewhere, aren't you? Hang onto the card the terminal prints out – a ticket to more bikes. When you reach your destination, just drop your bike off at the nearest Vélib rack.

The first 30 minutes are free; then it's 1 euro for the next half hour, 2 for the one after that, and €4 each successive half hour, so don't keep the bicycle for too long! Just drop it off, and pick up another bike using your card. You are charged €1 for 24 hours of privileges, and seven days cost €5.

**www.en.velib.paris.fr**

## Walking

Strolling Paris is the best way to appreciate the city, and you'll see that it's actually quite compact.  A few English-speaking walking-tour guides:

• Heather offers her own original take on whatever theme you suggest. Let your curiosity inspire you! Offbeat neighborhoods, food markets, bargain clothing, history, parks, flea markets and even... Naughty Paris (for Ladies).
**www.secretsofparis.com • 01 43 36 69 85**

• Strictly for foodies: one of the most appetizing tours we know of, with stops at landmark bakeries, caterers, cheesemongers, delicatessens, chocolate stores, markets, and tea rooms.
**www.parisexperiences.com**

> To download audio visits:
> **www.pocketvox.com**
> or www.soundwalk.com
> for audio visits (with
> personality!) of districts.

• A well-educated and friendly Indian woman will lead you through one of Paris's most exotic neighborhoods, La Chapelle, where one of the world's largest Tamil communities outside the subcontinent has settled. Shop the food markets with her spice advice, have a beauty treatment, choose bolts of silk for saris, just like in Bombay...
**Poonam Chawla: www.chalindia.com • 01 45 05 34 71 or 06 26 01 77 53**

• The well-trained guides at Paris Walks are skilled at making Paris come to life for you, whether they're talking about Louis XIV, the Da Vinci code, or chocolate - all encountered on the same tour.
**www.paris-walks.com.  01 48 09 21 40**

## Where is everyone?

Standard opening hours for shops are usually 9-10 am to 7-8 pm. Most close on Sunday, many close on Monday, and a few small ones shut down for lunch (12 to 2 pm, but neighborhood cheese shops, wine cellars, and produce stands may stay closed during the siesta hours from 1 to 4 or 5 pm). Please keep in mind that many places shut down in August. The bright side: bakeries and florist shops usually stay open all day Sunday, providing the essentials of life!

Because Parisians tend to sleep in on weekends, early Saturday and Sunday mornings are ideal for quiet, exploratory walks.

## How to face an emergency

Don't panic: France's health-care system is the best in the world. In case of a minor or major incident, just call the Fire Department (who have trained paramedics): dial 18. For Emergency (from a mobile phone): dial 112.

**Three drugstores are open 24 hours a day:**
**84 Avenue des Champs-Élysées, 8th • 01 45 79 53 19 ou 01 45 62 02 41**
**6 Place de Clichy, 9 th • 01 48 74 65 18**
**6 Place Félix-Éboué, 12th • 01 43 43 19 03**

**SOS Médecins (24h/24) makes house calls • 01 47 07 77 77**

## How to tip

A 15% tip is automatically included in the check in all restaurants, but people generally leave a little extra (a few euros will do) on the table, especially if the waiter was kind and patient, which is not always the case here.

## What about smoking?

If you were looking forward to puffing shamelessly on your Gauloise in typical Parisian fashion in cafés and restaurants, forget it! The government has recently banned smoking from all public places, which caused quite a stir. It's France, after all! Land of liberty! You are permitted to smoke on restaurant terraces, in the street, and even in parks. And non-smoking American musicians were getting suffocated when they played the clubs!

# Do they speak any English?

Most Parisians are highly literate people, so the ones you meet will probably speak English. Sometimes they'll be too uptight and embarrassed about their accents to try, though. For one reason or another, they are bound to make it as hard for you as possible, so do them the courtesy of using a few French words (use your rueful smile). This may coax them converse with you in English.

# The best places in town to meet English or American people, if you're homesick...

### American Church in Paris
CHURCH
**65 Quai d'Orsay, 7th • M° Invalides or Pont-de-l'Alma**

### Joe Allen
AMERICAN RESTAURANT
**30 Rue Pierre-Lescot, 1st • M° Étienne-Marcel**

### Breakfast in America
AMERICAN RESTAURANT
**17 Rue des Écoles, 5th • M° Cardinal-Lemoine or Jussieu**
**4 Rue Malher, 4th • M° Saint-Paul**

### Harry's Bar
AMERICAN RESTAURANT & BAR
**5 Rue Daunou, 2nd • M° Opéra**

# Conclusion

**Heading back already?** We hope that you enjoyed your second time around Paris. Like most visitors to the city, you must have fantasized about actually living here one day, above a café in the Latin Quarter, in an apartment overlooking the Seine, or in a loft in Belleville. Without knowing it, you may have crossed our path in the neighborhoods we love and live in. Now that the trip is over, we can admit it: we are staunch Right Bankers, who would not live on the other side of the Seine for anything in the world!

The best addresses are the ones you find yourself, and we'd love to hear from you about your explorations and discoveries: parigramme@parigramme.fr.

Have a particular interest in a subject like wine, antiques, fashion, beauty, terraces, or kissing? You'll find detailed information in English in the following Parigramme guides:

*Aux bons crus / Paris Wine Lovers' Companion*
*Paris déco*
*Paris chic & trendy*
*Paris Vintage*
*Paris Beauty*
*Paris Terrasses*
*The Best Places to Kiss in Paris*

www.parigramme.com

# Index

© **2008 Parigramme** / Compagnie Parisienne du livre (Paris)
www. parigramme.com

Édition / **Sandrine Gulbenkian** / **Mathilde Kressmann**
Direction artistique et réalisation / **Isabelle Chemin**

Révision et correction / **Anita Conrade** / **Lilith Cowan**

Achevé d'imprimer en octobre 2008 / **Kapp (Évreux)**

Dépôt légal / **novembre 2008**
ISBN / **978-2-84096-543-5**